THE
ART
OF
REDEMPTION

ALSO BY STUART WILDE

Books

Affirmations
The Force
God's Gladiators (published by Brookemark Publishing)
Infinite Self: 33 Steps to Reclaiming Your Inner Power
"Life Was Never Meant to Be a Struggle"
The Little Money Bible: The Ten Laws of Abundance
Miracles
The Quickening
The Secrets of Life
Silent Power
Simply Wilde: Discover the Wisdom That Is (with Leon Nacson)
Sixth Sense: Including the Secrets of the Etheric Subtle Body
The Three Keys to Self-Empowerment
The Trick to Money Is Having Some!
Weight Loss for the Mind
Whispering Winds of Change: Perceptions of a New World
Wilde Unplugged: A Dictionary of Life (e-book)

Audio Programs

The Art of Meditation
The Force (audio book)
Happiness Is Your Destiny
Intuition
"Life Was Never Meant to Be a Struggle" (audio book)
The Little Money Bible: The Ten Laws of Abundance (audio book)
Loving Relationships
Miracles (audio book)
Silent Power (audio book)

✦

All of the above are available at your local bookstore,
or may be ordered by visiting:

Hay House USA: www.hayhouse.com®
Hay House Australia: www.hayhouse.com.au
Hay House UK: www.hayhouse.co.uk
Hay House South Africa: orders@psdprom.co.za
Hay House India: www.hayhouse.co.in

THE
ART
OF
REDEMPTION

STUART WILDE

HAY HOUSE, INC.
Carlsbad, California
London • Sydney • Johannesburg
Vancouver • Hong Kong • New Delhi

Published and distributed in the United States by: Hay House, Inc.: www.
hayhouse.com • *Published and distributed in Australia by:* Hay House
Australia Pty. Ltd.: www.hayhouse.com.au • *Published and distributed in
the United Kingdom by:* Hay House UK, Ltd.: www.hayhouse.co.uk • *Published and distributed in the Republic of South Africa by:* Hay House SA
(Pty), Ltd.: orders@psdprom.co.za • *Distributed in Canada by:* Raincoast:
www.raincoast.com • *Published in India by:* Hay House Publishers India:
www.hayhouse.co.in

Stuart Wilde's editors: Lisa Kolbuc, Gillian Kenning
Editorial supervision: Jill Kramer
Design: Tricia Breidenthal

Library of Congress Cataloging-in-Publication Data

Wilde, Stuart.
   The art of redemption / Stuart Wilde. -- 1st ed.
     p. cm.
   ISBN-13: 978-1-4019-1754-8 (tradepaper) 1. Spiritual life. 2. Spirituality.
3. Redemption. I. Title.
   BL624.W537 2007
   299'.93--dc22   2006031522

ISBN 13: 978-1-4019-1754-8

10 09 08 07   4 3 2 1
1st edition, August 2007

CONTENTS

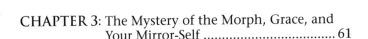

CHAPTER ONE

REDEMPTION
AND THE HOLY GRAIL

The Grail Mystery

This book talks about a strange mystery, a gap in reality that you can learn to walk through. Of all the Knights of the Round Table in the Camelot legend, only two found the Holy Grail. Perceval was one, and he later took over from the Fisher King to become the ruler of the Grail castle. Sir Galahad, known for his bravery and goodness, was the other knight who found the Grail. Both he and Perceval disappeared.

The wizard and prophet Merlin didn't have to find the Holy Grail because, in a way, he *was* the Grail. Eventually, he left the world of physical things and retreated into a crystal pyramid or cave in the forest. There he had a partner and helper, Nimue, who might have been his wife. She straddled the gap and went back and forth to the real world on Merlin's behalf. She, too, must have had a command of the Grail; otherwise, she wouldn't have been able to step from one dimension to another. Nimue was very special, as she was one of the Ladies of the Lake. She has always fascinated me, but sadly, I don't know enough about her to offer you any real information. But

1

she had the power according to the legend, and it was said that Merlin couldn't have operated from the forest without her.

Initially, the Grail was thought to be the cup that Jesus used at the Last Supper. Legend says that Joseph of Arimathea, who accepted Jesus's body from the Romans, carried the cup from the Middle East to Glastonbury, England. Later, the Holy Grail became known as the *sang raal* (the royal blood), sometimes written as the *sang real*. Books like *The Da Vinci Code* claim that Jesus was married to Mary Magdalene; and she and their child, a daughter, came to France by boat from Egypt along with Mary of Antioch. Also with them was the Black Madonna, an African woman who performed miracle healings and who was later revered as St. Sarah. They landed in the south of France at Saintes Maries de la Mer. The sang raal was said to be the bloodline of Jesus, Mary, and their descendants, who became the Merovingian kings of France, according to some claims.

These Grail legends of the cup and the holy bloodline of Jesus are intriguing stories, but beyond these possibilities is another that's much more tantalizing: It says that the Grail, shining with a great light, belongs in another world. And it's not so much a golden chalice, but a transdimensional doorway into another dimension. The Grail is a gap in reality in which humans can walk into, and they dematerialize when passing through it. Beyond the hidden door is a timeless world—the blissful state of an eternal now. What's pleasing about this third possibility is that it isn't limited to the restriction of a family bloodline or to stumbling across a chalice in southern England. It describes a spiritual state, the opening of the third eye, and a beautiful transformation of self that anyone can reach with tenacity and a nobility of heart.

Findley (1850), the American Camelot

So, are stories of the Grail and Camelot all myth, legend, stuff and nonsense—or is there some truth to it? Five years ago, I would've said that I don't know. My ol' teacher told me that the legend of the hidden door was real; and in the 1850s, there was an American Camelot called Findley that appeared in a valley in Nebraska. Many hundreds of people lived there, but it was invisible to others. On one occasion, according to my teacher, a stagecoach got lost in a storm and stumbled into Findley; the occupants of the coach stayed. After ten years or so, the transdimensional overlay that was the "Findley Camelot" melted, burst, or withdrew in some way, and the inhabitants walked out into the real world. It was a critical time in America as the Civil War (1861–1865) was looming.

Findley is a fascinating story, but of course, I had to take my teacher's word for it. However, since he told me about Findley some 25 years ago, I saw more and more visions and symbols during my spiritual journey that suggested the reality of one or more modern Camelots and the existence of the Grail doorway, which I later discovered isn't a myth after all. I found the hidden door that my teacher spoke of; and many times after that, I witnessed the dematerialization of the human body mentioned in the legend. So in the end, I was convinced. Ancient writings say that the old lamas in Tibet could walk through walls . . . I understand it better now.

Of course, to talk about dematerialization and walking through walls, I risk the fact that you might consider me utterly mad, but I would never lie to you, for I have no reason to rot my soul. And even through the tumult and inconsistencies of my own life, I also seek redemption. I wouldn't be qualified to talk about deliverance if I hadn't cared to make the journey myself. I also wouldn't want the bad karma of leading individuals astray, because I feel the single most important part of this great journey through life is to care for people.

If, at the end, I looked back and I hadn't at least tried to care tenderly for others' souls as best I could, my life would be nothing. I'm far too much of a spiritual wimp to risk that. When I set it all out later in these pages, you'll see that what I say is true: The hidden doorway of our redemption exists. Beyond it are dimensions so vast that this universe seems small and insignificant in comparison. In those worlds, you could easily hold the Milky Way in the palm of your hand! The door is there, and even if you're not quite ready, just approaching it evokes bliss because you can feel the reconciliation of self. It's the sensation of being made whole.

Parts that have been lost for eons come back to find you—it's a form of homecoming of the soul, a silent glory. The door does exist, and you'll find it if you care to as others have; it's a lot easier than you might imagine. I'll describe my experience and how the sight of the door first came about.

The Strange Phenomenon of Dematerialization

In March 2001, I was in the town of Milton, in New South Wales, Australia. Fifteen people were at my house when something very strange happened. We were sitting in the front room where there are a number of daybeds (like those very large, wide couches and sofas you see in movies in large Indian homes). Suddenly, a beautiful geometric pattern spontaneously appeared on one of the women's faces. It was circles and dots and triangles of many vibrant colors. They oscillated, moved, and shimmered across her face, spreading down her neck and covering her shoulders. It was both awesome and mysterious to watch.

There was no logical explanation for what was happening: No anomalous light effects in the room or sunlight from outside could cause the fractal, geometric forms that appeared on her skin. Further, the patterns were not static like a shadow might be; they undulated and sparkled and constantly changed positions. It was quite hot that afternoon, and one of the men had his T-shirt off, soon realizing that he too had the same kind of patterns forming on his back. Gradually over a period of 15 minutes or so, everyone had them on their bodies to some extent. Each configuration was different—some had blue stars, others had little red hearts, and some even had leopard-skin patterns—but they were all a manner of images and shapes clear to see.

This was the first time we ever experienced what later became known as the *Morph*. It's a phenomenon, a transdimensional overlay, whereby a room changes its imprint or ambience in the construct of space and time, and the surrounding reality takes on a new form. It's as if the room exists in two states: normal and solid looking, and abnormal and not solid at the same time. The walls appear to go soapy looking, and the floor seems to become hazy and unclear, disappearing even though you know you're standing on it. Hazy striations begin to swirl in the air, floating together to form vortices and circles that you imagine you can travel down—doorways calling you to another world.

What we found, to our amazement, was that even our bodies seemed to go from solid to not solid at all. I know this may sound very strange, but others and I have seen the Morph thousands of times since that first episode in 2001. The experience on that day wasn't a one-time event or a group hallucination, and I ought to add here that we weren't on anything dodgy like hallucinogenics or drugs of any kind. Everyone was stone-cold sober on that curious afternoon when the Morph first appeared.

I believe that the Morph represents a new world, a supernatural dimension descending on our 3-D world. I find it to be the ultimate transcendental experience, completely changing our view of spirituality and extra-sensory perception. The Morph is for you and me and everyone. You don't have to be specially trained to see it. I'll explain how you'll get there in a later chapter, but first let me finish the Morph story.

What we found on that day as the patterns appeared on our skin was that our heads and faces became less and less solid looking, and we could see the detailed bone structure of a person's head or hands through their skin as if looking at an x-ray. People's faces then started to go hazy, and parts of them would vanish completely, morphing into another dimension. At times we found that we could see right through each other; bits of us were dropping out of our everyday reality and disappearing.

It wasn't scary, just very intriguing. But when you first see that the world we so believe in isn't really solid at all, it befuddles your brain a little bit. It took us a while to comprehend the process. Then one of the guys realized that he could put his finger into another person's head and push it through the bone of the forehead into their skull. As he did it, we saw his finger dissipate inside the person's forehead; and when he finally pulled it out a minute or so later, it was elongated and pointed and slightly wet looking. We laughed, and then gradually everyone had the courage to try it. Eventually we found that we could put our hands and arms right inside of someone else's rib cage, and this person could feel a tickling sensation. We played this Morph game for four hours, like children with a new toy.

A day later, an upside-down Y appeared over a four-poster bed in one of the bedrooms in the house. When I put my hand up inside the crook of the Y, my hand and forearm just dematerialized. I couldn't see them anymore—all I had was a stump, so I decided to stand on the bed within the Y to see what would happen next. When I did that, it got a bit scary, as there was a tremendous upward-tugging sensation coming from the Y-shaped vortex. I felt that it might suck me off the bed and take me someplace I wasn't ready to go.

At that moment, other people in the house came into the room, and two of the guys held on to my legs. It made me feel safer, but I didn't stay up there for more than a few minutes because I was worried that the tugging sensation would get even stronger. Then one of the ladies took her turn to stand inside of the inverted Y, and we saw TV screens appear on her upper body, which were reflected on her clothes and skin as four-color images. Each was about one square foot, and pictures emerged on the screens, like video clips showing events regarding the destiny of the world. There were also images of galaxies and deep space and the outer universe. This lasted for about ten minutes, when she also felt the tugging sensation pulling her up, so she came down off the bed. After a couple of hours, ten people had a turn standing in the upside-down Y, and each partially dematerialized. (Later in this book I'll show you how to create a miniversion of the Y vortex, and you'll put the tip of your finger inside and watch it stretch and partially dematerialize. Then maybe you'll believe me, . . . " maybe not?)

Now let me move the story on quickly, for after those first two Morph events we found that it was everywhere all the time. When the Morph is very strong, you can see it even in bright daylight, but it's usually much easier to view in a darkened room. It often looks like dry rain with swirls and vortices in it. If you want to see it, you have to relax and learn to meditate if you don't already do so, for all the dimensions and experiences beyond this world call for the low brain-wave patterns of the meditative state.

In essence, the Morph is the doorway of the Holy Grail—for me, for you, and for all of humanity. In the legend, only two knights, Perceval and Galahad, got through, but now I believe that it's the destiny of thousands—if not tens of thousands—to make the journey. No one really knows why the Morph has appeared at this time. It's been said that it represents the descent of the goddess, who is here to preside over a transformation that will take the world from violence and its yang harshness to the yin gentility of the feminine spirit. There's validity to this idea, in that the Morph is very soft; it seems to have benevolent healing qualities of rejuvenation and rebirth.

Another process that's developed out of the Morph is the concept of finding the Grail doorway, which involves redemption and deliverance. It's the logical final step of a long spiritual journey whereby you redeem yourself, not only of your transgressions, but also of the stored memories of pain that you acquired in this life. It's the reconciliation of a noble soul, by which you're made whole to become part of an eternal higher order. It's as if you step through the doorway going from a very solid yang world to a more hazy yin one, and you do that in order to immerse yourself into another evolution. It's not death—it's peering through the door and learning, coming back to adjust what you already know and then returning to look some more.

Redemption offered by a priest or a religious system might be temporarily pleasing, worthy as a moment of enlightenment, say, but it doesn't wash away the wounds of a fragile soul, nor does it address the memories of past pain or the tarnished nature of one's journey through life. In truth, I doubt that anyone can instantly eliminate your sins; they're everlasting, just as your goodness is eternal.

Recovering the Extraordinary
Power of the Authentic You

I'm going to show you something empowering that's special and usually misunderstood or hidden away. Essentially, it's a journey beyond the confines of this reality, past what you've already experienced to a place reserved for you inside a hyperdimensional realm. There, you'll see the extraordinary power of what's come to be known as the "authentic you." It's in the authenticity of your true spirit that reconciliation lies.

Normally we live in what might be a confined, rather fake, humdrum existence with little inspiration regarding the future. It's often blank and linear, created by the intellect and the desires of the ego. I'd like to discuss how to step off that lonely, narrow path and peer into another world—a magnificent world of transdimensional beings and helpers, and the potential of a "superknowing" that isn't limited by false boundaries of what's sometimes an egocentric perception of life.

There *is* a mirror-world to this one. In the late 1920s, English physicist Paul Dirac first discovered it mathematically as an "antiparticle" world. Later his theory was confirmed: Every particle has an antiparticle of the opposite charge, and those particles form a mirror-world to this one. Part of the journey here is the story of that mirror-world, how to see it, and what to do in order to help yourself once you're aware of these other worlds. It's up to you to decide how little or how much you feel you can use for guidance.

The Invisible You

In essence, this is all about the "invisible" you, the one that normally can't be seen, which is where your supernatural power lies. It's akin to the Taoist concept of gazing at the spaces between the leaves of a tree as well as the actual tree. It's all about what's in the gap and how you'll learn to peer into it, eventually walking through. Once you are in there with a settled heart, looking back at the world, you'll never see life in the same way again. You'll find that much of the struggle and pain falls away, and your life is bathed in a higher light. It's the voyage beyond enlightenment, but it isn't the acquiring of new rules; rather, it's letting go of old ones and dogma to become more liberated. Many thousands have seen the gap that I speak of, and the Morph stands at its threshold. If you put your hand into the gap, it dematerializes. This

isn't an airy-fairy concept; certainly one would say that it's a path less traveled, but a very real one, nonetheless.

First you have to get the door to appear to you by calling on the celestial forces for help. Your soul is soft and feminine and way more delicate than your waking mind; and while the intellect may be strong and aligned to the world of yang and the masculine force that conquers and prospers in a commercial world, the invisible you thrives in the inner worlds from gentility and tenderness. For all healing comes from this yin energy, which the Tao calls the feminine spirit, or the valley spirit. It's in the softness that you'll redeem yourself, and it's in the breadth of the compassion for who you are that you eventually embrace absolution and reconciliation.

The quintessential beauty of this spiritual journey through the gap is that you can take as long as you wish and go as far as you'd like—even going just a little way allows you to formulate a new perspective. Then, you can come back to the path ten years later if you want. I know people who started 20 years ago and are now very metaphysically sophisticated, but they probably needed that time. Those who came later started higher up the ladder with less clutter and more inner power; and in the end, there will be people who can just walk into the gap of this mysterious femininity that I speak of and they'll instantly see the door.

The Fringe Dwellers

I've come to believe that certain people have a special karma, a destiny to transcend, and that deep inner feeling puts them on the edge of society. I call these individuals the *fringe dwellers*. These aren't hippy revolutionaries or New Age space cadets, for the fringe dwellers are set apart only in that they think differently. There's a spiritual energy that calls to them from a long way off, causing them to question and wonder.

You might have been working in a humdrum (what I call "tick-tock") job at the post office for 40 years, but in your mind you don't quite belong to these systems. You know that you're a citizen of a far country, a part of a spiritual consciousness that doesn't tally much with the regular, everyday mind-set. It makes you different, not special necessarily; it's just that you're not aligned to the way the world thinks. Being on the fringe can sometimes cause pain and difficulty, especially if you fight it, for its inherent contradictions can cause confusion and listlessness.

I realized that I didn't fit in at an early age. I was raised in Africa without television; and at the age of ten, I was shipped off to an austere English boarding school that was like a prisoner-of-war camp. We called it Stalag 14. There, I had to pretend to be an upper-crust Englishman, but the truth was I was neither upper crust nor English. I was a little African kid, albeit a white African kid. I knew nothing about the outlook or the ideals of a gentleman and his pleasures (like rugby and cricket) and other strange games and rituals that I'd never seen before. I knew how to catch a barracuda and how to grind cassava, and I knew a bit about which snakes are poisonous and which aren't, but that wasn't very useful on the playing fields of England.

That's where my fringe-dweller mentality started. Around the age of 12, I formed a small alternative society. There were about a dozen of us lost boys. We lived in the roof of the school's gymnasium, and getting there was a perilous journey across narrow iron girders to reach the gap between the ceiling and the outside roof of the building. Once in that magical, hidden world, you had to watch your step because if you missed an iron joist that held the ceiling up, you'd fall through to the gym floor 20 to 30 feet below. I lived in that roof with my pals on and off for five years, and we spent every spare moment of our school days there. We never plotted to destroy the system—just to survive it. School was a very nasty, violent place, but we found that if we stuck together and pooled our resources, we could not only get by but also thrive. It was a sanctuary, but it was also a state of mind. This was my first understanding of the feminine spirit. We created a place of compassion with the combined effort of like-minded scalawags.

We got 2 shillings and 6 pence pocket money each week, which at today's exchange rate is about 23 cents U.S. But in clubbing our meager capital, we realized that we could buy stuff that the other boys wanted—candy, food, and so on—and so we'd sell them their heart's desire at a small but well-deserved profit. In this way our little society of schoolboy fringe dwellers prospered, and we felt free and safe, living in the roof away from prefects and masters and teachers who would beat us with a stick at the lightest excuse. We were quick, agile, and fairly fearless. We could run across the narrow beams that reinforced the roof in seconds, even in the dark—and so we never got caught, not once in five years.

The interesting thing is that the young boy who lived in the roof was the authentic me, the benevolent and sensitive one, sharing and helping others. On the other hand, the boy who was on the playing fields, hopelessly pretending to be an English gentleman, was the fake, competitive me—an image that was thrust upon me. We all suffer from an enforced conformity. It's a mind-control disease that enables society and our families to legislate over us, trapping us in their mental prisons. It's ghoulish, really.

In my 20s, my mother, who was a great believer in spiritualism and mediumship, gave me a book called something like the *Powers That Be*. It was all about spirit realms and the hierarchies of angels who guide those who seek a higher perception. Suddenly, I saw that there was a possible way out of this harsh world to a spiritual one. Indeed, there was a safe place for those who didn't fit— another "gymnasium ceiling" to discover and perhaps hide within. To realize that these things were possible at such a young age was an enormous impetus for me. One of my friends, who's very transdimensional in his softness and thinking, told me that he could remember knowing that he was a fringe person at the age of three.

Think back and you'll probably remember when you first knew it for yourself. Maybe it was a dream you had as a small child, or perhaps it was something you saw—a sacred symbol, for instance. Or, did you experience the fleeting vision of angels or transdimensional beings in your home? I believe that this recognition is an imprint on your soul, an ancient memory meant to remind you that no matter what happens in this life, you belong to a faraway land. Your true home is a dimension beyond fear and pain, a place of honor and nobility—a realm to which one day you're destined to return.

In the immaturity of my youth, I struggled with the fringe-dweller idea so I drifted into moneymaking, self-importance, glamour, and foppish things—nonsenses that made up the rickety scaffolding of my naive sense of self. I was perpetually trying to fit while not fitting at the same time. It was all a bit ludicrous. (You might have tried it; it's terribly difficult.) Eventually, I saw that being a fringe dweller is just fine as long as you're not plotting to burn down city hall. It's permissible to be an outsider and to seek the society of others who also don't conform. It's fine to travel and leave it all behind, embarking on a great voyage of discovery: a quest to find the freedom of the real you. To that end, it's okay to build your own relationship with God, rather than borrowing one from others or having one imposed upon you by a system of control or an institution.

If you've ever experienced the fringe-dweller perception and you've noticed the way it carries you off into strange places, then you'll know what it's like to be marginalized. Congratulate yourself on having held on to the authentic you in spite of the unfavorable odds. At least you've survived, and the doorway out of here isn't far ahead. I made it my life's mission to find the hidden door that my teacher spoke of, for I felt that the celestial worlds would treat me better than this one. And anyway, the world of the mundane got on my nerves—I found it repetitive and lifeless. After about 30 years of trial and error and a few spooky dead ends, the Morph arrived in the spring of 2001 . . . and there was the door—*click*.

It's a threefold process: There's the Morph and the sight of it; the ennoblement of the Grail, which I'd describe as the gift of a heightened perception within a newfound softness; and finally, the process of deliverance and redemption. The third part is tricky, as it involves a journey through your subconscious shadow. I won't deal at length with this concept now; suffice it to say that you have a mirror-self that is one with your shadow-self. Discovering the shadow is part of the process of understanding the authentic total you.

Perceval's Journey to the Grail

In searching for the Grail castle, Perceval found himself on the banks of a river and couldn't figure out which way to go. We all suffer indecision at some point on our path. We get bogged down in ideas and concepts, processes, and sacred writings or religious dogma; we spin and spin, finding no way forward.

A ferryman came and offered to take Perceval across the water. In the legend, the ferryman was in disguise, for he's actually the Fisher King, ruler of the Grail castle. He sets Perceval on the right path and then says to him, "Have a care lest the wood misleads you, for that would but please me."

The wood is the ego, whereby we sense the Grail up ahead and get lost in self-importance or take to ideas of specialness. That's the cult of the *Chosen One* when one erroneously believes that he or she has been selected to save humanity. Eventually, Perceval arrives at the Grail castle. He washes the rust of his armor from his body, and he's given silken clothing to wear, symbolizing purity. A banquet is held in his honor; and the queen, Rapanse de Schoye, brings out the Holy Grail, which shines in the room like the light of God. Perceval must solve a riddle in order to claim it, but he doesn't know the answer, so the Grail is taken away. All of the ladies and courtiers of the castle withdraw.

Perceval is forced to leave, and as he crosses the draw-bridge of the castle, the gatekeeper calls out to him, say-ing, "Thou art a goose, henceforth thou shall see only dark." This means that we can all arrive at the Grail in our minds; and yet, if our darkness is still hidden from us, unredeemed and still in place, we don't possess the nobility with which to claim it. Perceval then went on a long, tortuous journey, fighting various battles before he was able to return and claim the Holy Grail and become the king of the Grail castle.

The worlds beyond the door protect themselves and won't let you in if you still carry a hidden darkness. For if evil could penetrate the celestial worlds, the angelic beings who reside there would have to give ground and withdraw farther back. Each unprocessed human carries with them not only their own darkness, but also etheric entities that hover close by for heat. If those beings slip past, there'd be hell to pay. They're stuck here with us on this side of the door . . . and that's the way the celestial likes it.

Here are photos of a partial dematerialization of the human body, just so you know that I'm speaking the truth.

Bob Trollinger

A shaman (Kajuyali Tsamani) in Brazil partly disappears.

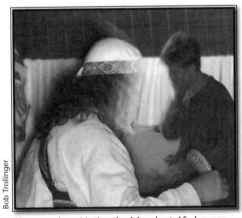

Bob Trollinger

Close-up shot. Notice the Morph at 45 degrees.

A partial dematerialization at the house in Milton, Australia. (Note that the other man is still solid.)

It's hard to acquire a photo of the dematerializations, as you can't set up the shot—you have to get it at exactly the right moment. But they *are* real, and they're part of where this mystical journey has arrived so far. As I talk to you about the gap and what lies in there for you to see and experience, just keep an open mind and trust me a little bit—without of course, ever giving up any of your own reality.

This is a shortcut that I offer, but it takes a bit of discipline and the will to succeed. There's the defined benefit that I mentioned as you reclaim the authentic you, which in its initial state is holy, sacred, and good. Most of the struggle in life comes from holding up the fake you and

striving in a world of yang rules and ideals. It's through your feminine spirit that you create your own secret heaven in the gymnasium's roof of your soul. You take the journey that the lords and ladies of the Grail took to establish the authentic you; and while doing that, you can agree to be a proud fringe dweller.

In the end, you have to make peace with all of humanity even within what are often very restrictive, controlling systems that have enormous power over you. Silently, you can wander off in your mind and your soul like Perceval, and eventually you belong to something else. That's the story of the redemption that I discuss here. And yes, it's a psychological and spiritual process, but it's also a real place, a dimension that permeates the very spot where you're now reading this book. It's just a few feet away from you at 90 degrees.

THE JOURNEY BEYOND ENLIGHTENMENT

The journey beyond enlightenment is essentially the voyage that surpasses the ego's insecurities, its incessant demands, and the stress that it creates in your life. Fear is a part of the ego's prison. It drives you to act strangely, but you can change that. The world of the ego isn't an authentic one, so gradually you have to melt it in order to return to the true self, which is your absolute beauty and identity. It's the eternal that you coupled with the power of knowing yourself. By that, I mean your spiritual identity, not just your name and your physical body, but who you are. Ask yourself, *What strange place did I come from? What is my life's mission?*

That is . . .

- Who are you?
- What are you doing here?
- What purpose do you serve?

Once you can answer these questions, you disappear—well, sort of. It's as if everything you think you are, your personality, and all that you know and hold dear (your life's story)—the very memory of you—dissolves.

And at the very end of the journey, there's nothing there, just an eternal silence and a sense of indescribable beauty and awe.

It sounds strange, eerie even, but in fact, it's beautiful because once you go past all the various definitions of "you," you'll also leave behind the pain, which is hooked or linked as an attached file to the icon that describes your identity. If you delete the old icon, the hurt goes to the recycling bucket; and suddenly in that lightness of being, you remember who you are and what your life's mission is if you don't already know it. You'll see yourself beyond terms of enlightenment and the arrogance of ignorance. Finally, you'll know the secret, which will bring you great joy. It changes your etheric imprint—the overall resonance of you and your life.

You're a recording—a digital imprint that you make on life that can bring healing not only to you and your loved ones, but also to humanity in general. And you won't necessarily have to hang a shingle on your door advertising your opening hours, as that may be too limiting. If your resonance is right, you'll only have to walk past people and they'll begin to heal. To change your resonance is to alter the vibration of the world ever so slightly. We'll talk more about the resonance of your soul in Chapter 4.

We're defined by what we think we are because it makes us feel safe. So, we work hard to become Harry the doctor, Mrs. So-and-So, the mother, the social worker, the teacher, and so on. These are evolutions of the mind, but it can be a tiring and limiting experience to play out the role you or others have selected. This is because your whole existence is framed in definitions that aren't actually real; they're just emotional, intellectual clusters that you belong to, groupings of a singular mind-set. Beyond the gap you are vast and eternal; and all of the silly rules and restrictions will eventually melt and become meaningless and unimportant, for you're destined to arrive at the infinite you. You'll enter into an eternity of all things where human titles, stuff, and even the body have no special meaning.

It's in the losing of the "you" that you think is authentic when you eventually arrive at the "new" you. The human identity that contained so much fear and suffering is replaced by a boundless version of you, connected to everything and part of an eternal order, including all the primal forces, spirits of nature, angelic beings, and every manner of wonderfulness that exists beyond the memory of stored anguish (old images in your subconscious mind or soul).

Then the connection you make is one of pure contentment, and the honor and reconciliation of that is the Grail—beyond light and dark or solid and not solid. It's the fusion of your anima or animus, a deliverance from evil, to a place where you hover as nothing and everything at the same time. It's quirky to think of, but once you let go of what you think you are and the definitions that you created for yourself, then you can become everything. It's the bliss of belonging once more—the joy of remembering.

A Journey to the Void

One day in France in August 2001, I found myself in the mirror-world in my etheric self, going down a tube that I couldn't see properly. The sensation had started spontaneously while I was out shopping. It was so unnerving that I had to return to my hotel room and lie down. The tube I felt was very tight and suffocating and uncomfortable, and I didn't have a clue what was happening to me. I was rather scared. There was a terrible crushing sensation on my chest that accompanied the journey down, which eventually lasted for more than eight hours. At times, I really believed that I was finished—I feared my heart would stop. The problem was that I couldn't prevent myself from sliding down the tube, so enduring the process was my only option.

The reason I mention this story is that as I went down the tube, I had to say good-bye to everything I held dear: life, family, my partner, and so on. I didn't know if I was ever coming back. I had to trust in the unseen and cast myself to the wind, so to speak, for I couldn't understand what was happening, nor could I see the tube that was squeezing me so tightly I could hardly breathe. It was a threshold experience for me, as I had to surrender and give it all away in order to arrive someplace else.

About four hours into the journey, something else mind-boggling happened: I began to hear a faint noise emanating from my chest just below my ribs on the right side. It was the voice of a child. The voice grew louder and louder and kept calling to me, saying, "Help me, help me!" It was pitiful. I had no idea where the child was or how I was supposed to help. It caused me to feel a tremendous amount of helplessness and emotional stress added to what I was already going through. (Since then, I've heard the child's voice many times over the last five years, and I've been able to record it twice. On one occasion, I taped it repeatedly saying, "Love me, love me." Others have listened to it, too, so I know that it's not a mind game or an aberration of my perception.)

I felt terrible. It was late at night and dark within the tube, and I couldn't help the little one. But I was in a life-and-death situation of my own, so I had to abandon my concern for the child and concentrate instead on trying to breathe while enduring the crushing sensation. Intellectually, I decided that I was inside a gravitational singularity, as if passing through a black hole in space, but I couldn't figure out how it could be present in 3-D, in a hotel room in France. I was intensely worried all the way.

A silver ball appeared far away in the distance. I watched as it gyrated on its axis, wobbling back and forth at great speed. Over several hours it got closer and closer, and I had difficulty coping with the inevitability of its approach. I noticed the gravitational anomaly that I felt was near or around the silver ball, and it began to make my leg shake uncontrollably, like a spasm. Soon my whole body shook violently, reminding me of an epileptic writhing on the floor during a seizure. At times the spasms were so strong they lifted me off the bed, as my back arched and my arms and legs flayed about, pulsing with the most horrible, uncontrollable violence.

It's dark, I'm scared, the child is crying for help, and I can do nothing. My body is lurching like a madman's, and I can't breathe from the increasing pressure of the invisible tube . . . you'd think nothing else could go wrong! But there was one more component still to come. About five hours into this, I became aware that I was under attack from a force (or forces) I also couldn't see. All I could discern in my mind's eye was what looked like hundreds of dirty snowballs crossing through space and coming toward me. There was no way to avoid them—there were too many. When the snowballs exploded, they did so on the outside of my energy, say, a few feet from my physical body. Each explosion buffeted me; it was like being violently shoved from behind. It reminded me of old war films when anti-aircraft fire detonates close to a bomber, shaking the plane with the force of each explosion. Most of the attack seemed to be directed toward my lower back in the area of my kidneys. The pounding of the concussions was disturbing, but they weren't individually painful. But as the hits mounted, I became more and more troubled, and I wasn't sure how much longer I could endure before surrendering.

After about two more hours the ack-ack fire stopped, and I entered a place of reasonable calm. I couldn't hear the child anymore, which was a blessing, as its plaintive cries broke my heart. But in the meantime, the crushing sensation had exacerbated tenfold. I couldn't expand my chest to take a breath, so I sucked air in through my teeth in very small sips. But it wasn't enough, and I felt that I'd faint.

I made a point of surrendering to death in those extreme circumstances; it was the only noble way in which to proceed. The first stanza of Rupert Brooke's beautiful poem "The Soldier" came to mind, and I recited the lines over and over. The words made me cry, but they also offered solace in a bittersweet sort of way.

If I should die, think only this of me:
That there's some corner of a foreign field
That is for ever England. There shall be
In that rich earth a richer dust concealed;
A dust whom England bore, shaped, made aware,
Gave, once, her flowers to love, her ways to roam,
A body of England's, breathing English air,
Washed by the rivers, blest by suns of home.

After about eight hours, I popped out of the oppressive tube and found myself in a great void. The pressure was gone. It was a huge relief, but this new place was also very daunting, deep in the width of its silence. It's jolly hard to convey the emptiness, as there's nothing concrete to describe. Imagine hovering in outer space and all you see is a thick darkness—no stars and no light. Every direction you look in is exactly the same; all views are meaningless. It's as if you're floating in a brand-new, unformed universe, and you're the only one there: no signpost, no one to question, and no higher beings present who might assist you. You can hear no sounds, just a timeless silence—an eternity of nothing.

There isn't a suitable word in English to describe the state of beyond panic, but *panic-plus-plus* might suffice. It was white terror, accompanied with a deep sense of devastation and loneliness. But the real worry for me was, "How the hell do I get out of this void?" While there, I had no comprehension of the experience ever ending, as there was no concept of time—ten minutes could've been days. There was just an awful feeling of being stranded with absolutely no clues or help whatsoever. It was a terrible case of utter abandonment.

Normally when you're stuck for an answer, you should always rely on your feelings, not logic, since they usually know how to get you out of a mess. So, I did just that in the void. I tried to sense what direction might be the best, but the problem was that in a void, your feelings don't have anything to glob on to. There's no defined energy to read or perceive. It was double the panic, as my trusted guiding system, ESP and intuition, had been taken from me.

I don't know how long I was in the void since there was no way to measure time. I began praying to Jesus (which felt gloriously silly, as I'm not a Christian), and I called on the spirits of eternity to help me. Nothing happened for a long while, but then something bloody marvelous did occur. I became aware of a faint tugging sensation in the center of my back that gradually grew stronger, and then I was sucked backward through an L-shaped flip, and then another L-shaped flip; and suddenly, I was back in my body in my hotel room.

There was a piano at the foot of my bed, and I thought that if I could use it to haul myself along, I could reach the spa bath in the corner of the room and recover. But as I got off the bed, my legs weren't all there, and I fell to the ground. I couldn't see my legs—*beaucoup de panic* added to all the previous terror. I started to crawl very slowly across the floor, using the piano's legs to pull myself up on my elbows and move toward the bath. It took a long time. Finally, I saw my legs morph back into view, and that encouraged me a whole lot. I was exhausted but managed to clamber over the edge of the bath. I stayed in the water for a couple of hours and fell asleep. It was past dawn when I woke up, and I could hear birds outside in the garden. I've never been so grateful for their song in all of my life; the little birds tore at my soul and made me cry.

I'm not sure why I took that journey in the mirror-world down the tube and into the void; I'm not saying that you'll also have to go, but if you do, it's an amazing gift. When you return, you see the utter joy of not being alone in this world. There are animals and birds and people, waves and tides and rain and storms, and corn wafting in lush fields. There's a pint of Guinness on a countertop somewhere, waiting for me and you. Life is rich and abundant with people, energy, feelings, colors, and things.

I know this story of the void may sound terribly strange, but billions have experienced the same journey going the other way but don't remember it. If you were born via a natural birth, not a cesarean one, you exited the darkness of your mother's womb and traveled down an excruciatingly tight, scary tunnel—the birth canal—into the light. My voyage was not so different, except I went from the light of this world through the tunnel back to the source, which is the void of another world.

I've told you this because it's a story of surrender. Pause and imagine that you're in the void, and there's nothing—no family or friends, no sounds, no up or down, no hope, just blankness. Look down and see the infinite darkness below. You could ask in a meditation, *Show me the void,* but you'll have to hang on to your hat if beings come to honor your request.

Looking back at my experience in France, I've always been a bit proud, as I proved to myself that I'd give up everything to reach the other side. It's a feeling of being small and frail and troubled by the enormity of things, but it's also a sense of being authentic and whole inside a fragile mortality. It's the journey from the fake you to the real you. The void revealed that; it taught me to be more grateful.

The Story of Om and Ka

Here's a legend of the void that's very sweet. In the beginning there was a vast space; it was beautiful, but it was dark and cold and wide. The space was feminine, and the Higher Gods called her *Om.* Light was also present; it was blisteringly hot because it was held in a confined

29

space. The light was masculine, and his name was given as *Ka*. Om thought that she would die because she was freezing and lonely, and Ka also believed that death was near, as he was so restricted and hot.

He said to Om, "Why don't you let me fly around your space? I can warm you and provide light; and in doing so, I can cool myself down because you're so beautiful and vast." She agreed, so Ka flew around the great emptiness of Om. She saved him from the extreme heat, and he in turn rescued her from the cold. Both had a deep love for each other and were grateful. From the union of Om and Ka, came their children, which we know as the stars and galaxies high above us. And from the dust of those stars, came the grandchildren of Om and Ka, who came to be known as humans.

After many eons passed, Om and Ka were both very old. Ka said, "We have trillions of wonderful children, but I'm old and have no heat left." Om loved all the children, but she also knew that she was tired and could expand her space no further. So, the two of them went hand in hand, returning to the source from whence they came, taking their children with them. They knew precisely where they all were, leaving no one behind.

Male and female and birth and rebirth are the teachings of Om and Ka, and that's the message of the void. We're a microcosm of our celestial parents. The human version of Ka is in the form of man's sperm, and a woman's womb is Om, the void.

The Ivory Tower

Let's talk about how to become more authentic and how you'll turn your evolution to go the other way, for that will empower the marriage of masculine and feminine and light and dark within you. It will show you the way to reconciliation, but you might need that flip of perception before you can access it.

For many, life is confusing, scary, and rather brutal at times—a painful journey through the unknown, where human predators lurk. You must work very hard and compete fiercely to make ends meet, often faced with every rule and situation stacked against you. To counteract the fear and struggle of all this, the ego builds the psychology of an ivory tower for you to live in. The ego feels safe there and protects you from dealing with people intimately and experiencing hurt and disappointment. You're now raised in your mind—above the crowd. From there, you can gaze down on humanity through your separation and imagined specialness, assuring yourself that the destiny of ordinary people isn't your fate. And you might also decide that you've been elevated and chosen and made exceptional. That's what the ego likes: to be higher and distanced from others and to feel glamorous and be noticed, which makes the ivory tower more real.

That's why people boast and show off, making elaborate stories of their minor achievements. They're seeking recognition and status—a greater altitude for their ivory tower. The electricity of the ego sustains the tower. The more power a person has, the more temperamental, capricious, and self-centered they can be. The impulsive, demanding pop star is an example of the ego's electricity running rampant. They use their moodiness to sustain the tower of their importance and their divinelike status. They need constant attention and input. The ego drives people to seek prestige and a positioning over others— including glitzy stuff, flashy cars, the red carpet, and the VIP lounge—in order to attract the spotlight.

The tower is sustained by the biophotons of the etheric, which we generate in part by self-importance and some of the electricity we get from the recognition of others. They transfer energy through their concentration on us or by their positive emotional response—the adulation of fans, say.

And through the incoming energy from others, the ego falsely elevates itself, desiring center stage. We seek electricity, external energy sources, to sustain us and help us feel safe and less vulnerable. That illusion of specialness comes from the personality's sense of separation, but it often comes at a terrible price; for in the isolation of elitism and the ivory tower, you become ever so slightly mad. The voltage of the tower fries your senses in the end, and you'll require more and more of it to keep the illusion going.

This blinds you to reason, as you see only your own mind, ideals, terms, and definitions. The other six billion people here are more or less irrelevant except for how they might feed the ego's need. You're on the top of the tower with an old, rusty gun marching up and down, guarding the edifice of your mind-set. It doesn't really matter if it's tiring you out or gradually killing you, as long as you're king or queen and can shut out pollution in the form of contradictions of the ego and/or the presence of other humans with new ideas. Of course, the madman or madwoman at the top isn't actually any safer than anyone else—the tower's height is an illusion, and protection is arbitrary at the very least.

This is because the tower costs time, money, and stress to maintain it. You have to buy a car that's perhaps more than you can afford, and maybe you live in a place that's too expensive. Then, there are all the other trappings that must be financed, for the ego will want this, then that, and then another thing; and soon you are its slave, rushing about trying to fill its every desire. So, although you're the king or queen of the castle on the tower with your rusty gun, you're actually a prisoner of stress and your ideals—psychologically and spiritually trapped. And being up there can make you lonely and isolated, and usually you'll become cold even though you may pretend to be social and warm; in fact, you see everyone as dispensable and may treat them with disdain and indifference.

Your ego acts as the Ministry of Authorized Information. It's up in the madhouse, and anyone who contradicts the edicts is due for annihilation or will be banished from your world. People who challenge information that you hold to be true must be proved wrong and belittled. This is the control mechanism of the demonic side of humankind. It's our attempt to impose ourselves onto others. We know best, for we're divinely selected—the chosen ones. All others must be heretics and heathen because they don't agree with us, and of course, they can't be quite as special as the fool on the roof, who's destined to be very important and different. As you might have already guessed, redemption comes in the end with the collapse of the tower.

The Embracing of a New Liberty

Something I learned early on in my journey is that much of the stuff we believe is fed to us backward. I wrote about this strange phenomenon at great length in my book *God's Gladiators,* where I talk about spiritual beings who are here to fight on our behalf. For example, we've been told that hell is hot, but if you've ever seen the demonic worlds, you soon realize that they're cold, austere, and bleak. Hell is freezing and soul-less, and the dark energies in there are terribly ugly. The celestial world is warm and comfortable, filled with radiant colors, kind sentiments, and a gentle compassion that comes from beautiful souls. In case you don't believe me, pause and think of someone who's very analytical and cerebral, and then touch him or her with your feelings; you'll feel the cold, clammy nature of their spirit—frozen glue. Then think of a person who's a bit crazy, funny, and less inhibited, and you'll bask in the warmth—champagne. That's the difference: Heaven is warm, but hell and its ghosts are cold, wet, and dank; and humans who are elitist and dogmatic are frigid.

If you've led an unpleasant, rather egocentric life focusing just on yourself, you now have the opportunity to reverse your perspective and join the party, becoming something different. When you're cold and vindictive and competitive, you enter into a ghoulish dimension where chilly, unseen beings gather around you. They reflect what you are. In life, the imprint of your very last feelings always surrounds you; and on an energy level, you're drifting between heaven and hell all the time without realizing it. (If it's confusing, you'll understand better when we discuss the mirror-world and your identity in there in later chapters.)

You may be familiar with the work of Dr. Masaru Emoto, the Japanese professor who photographs frozen water crystals. He'd hold a test tube of water and write the word *Hitler* on it, say, and then he'd freeze it and take pictures of the water crystals, which would come out all demonic looking. Then, he'd repeat the process but write the word *joy* on the tube, and the crystals would take the form of a beautiful snowflake. Professor Emoto's pioneering work really highlights the effect we have on our surroundings and the way we each make an imprint on life—for better or worse.

Almost all of your body is water—you're a mobile puddle—and whatever you think and feel is imprinted into your energy just as Emoto's crystals are affected by emotion. All the resonance or information travels around with you, warping reality to a new ugliness—or healing it, depending on how you feel and express yourself minute by minute. When you're warm and tactile and genuinely care for humanity from your heart, you push away the imprint of the negative, dark beings and draw the beginnings of a celestial dimension closer to you. A miniheaven on Earth walks around with you; it's easy to work out. To love people and include them is to silently offer them approval, so you could say that it's the offer of reconciliation and redemption. When you're freezing, you exclude people, condemning them as lesser beings. Sometimes you seek domination or authority over others, or your coldness desires vengeance, wishing others ill. When you go frigid, you fall into the arms of the demonic, which claims you as its own—*spooky-dooky.*

Now here's something about the iciness of emotions that's can be seen in the Morph. It's quite interesting, and few people know about it. In the mirror-world that we view through the lens of the Morph, we see feelings acting as mini-dimensions. They're actual places—geographies, I call them. Cruelty, for example, is exemplified in physical acts, or it's a psychological state of mind, but it's also a sentiment of self-importance—a feeling of disdain for others. It's a dark trip often involving reprisals. And while cruelty is all of these things and more, it's also a vector in the mirror-world, a direction in hyperspace, and a place you can travel to.

If you're facing north, as if standing in the center of a compass, and you could slide through the hidden door into the mirror-world from that center spot, you'd head to your left toward the point that's marked by 260 degrees on the compass (almost directly west from you). You'd also notice that you're going down through the floor at a very slight angle of 17 degrees. Within minutes of traveling sideways and downward in that direction, you'll find yourself surrounded by the Lords of Cruelty and all the collective cruelty that humans have for each other and the animal kingdom. The emotion of cruelty is at a specific location, as well as being a facet sometimes hidden in the minds of men and women.

Interestingly, love is not contained in any one place. It's spread out like a wash of violet color across an evening sky. Cruelty defines your geography because of a loveless state of mind, but love expands you. It's a thin layer of eternity, allowing you to be everywhere rather than the excruciatingly tight dimension that's located at 260 degrees left and 17 degrees down. I know where it is because I was taken there once to see it as part of my lessons. It was worse than bloody awful . . . not a holiday destination that I'd recommend.

People don't realize that in the silence of their thoughts and feelings, they condemn themselves to exist in hellish dimensions, invisibly surrounded by others who are as dark as they are. It's unsettling, of course, as those bottled thoughts pull dangerous humans to you, psychopaths who glory in manipulation and influence.

The allure of the dark is intoxicating, for it offers the illusion of unbridled power that comes from the use of fear and control. We all fall prey to those sentiments at times, as the ego likes dominion over others because it offers the false notion of immortality. In that lust for power, it seeks an eye for an eye, a tooth for a tooth, and all that sounds pleasing to the ego. But that is the loveless world of the phony self; there, you can find justification for all sorts of nastiness and silent crimes against humanity. It takes a brave person to go the other way and offer forgiveness instead of seeking vengeance.

You might think that salvation comes from being special and chosen and part of some elitist system, but it's rather dark. It often involves a false sense of ethnic superiority or the illusion of social status, always excluding others. In fact, deliverance comes from being ordinary and human and not needing to be special—drop that and you're already walking in the right direction. Part of the reverse perception that I speak of is hard to see, for we're often preprogrammed to seek satisfaction and the attention of others. But it's often a futile quest, as the more you search for approval, the less people will offer it because they're usually mesmerized in attaining their own. You don't need the disappointment of it all. The right direction is to become humble and sensitive toward others. Rather than asking how life will sustain you, you should start to think of how you might serve humanity if you don't already do so.

Spiritual empowerment, the journey beyond enlightenment, liberates you from the need to be special, releasing you from the effort of supporting the ivory tower and the unquenchable need to acquire more. Watching TV is funny: You'll see one guy who claims that he's the world's greatest hippopotamus catcher, and you're thinking, *yeah, yeah*—you're on the side of the hippo hoping for lunch. Then, another fool claims that he's the most amazing bounty hunter, another is the fastest running back, here's the most talented chef; and there are a whole host of the world's best rappers, hip-hoppers, flip-floppers, and those who make the incredible shots on the basketball court. In the end, what do we have? Just mad fools on the ivory tower, calling out to the heavens saying, "I'm the greatest, the king (or queen) of the castle, and I'm squeaky clean and special and different. You lot below me are dirty rascals, destined for a terrible end. You'll all wither and die as insignificant nobodies, while I'll be forever immortalized in my deeds and my hippo-catching wonderfulness, fully anointed by God. That's what *I* am!"

The trick is to eventually arrive at nothing and not be the world's greatest anything. You don't need it—free your mind. And if you're the world's best something, there's never a reason to tell anyone . . . is there? I learned that the simple thing is to retreat from competing and to step back into the silence and comfort of just knowing. It's best to let all those on the tower push and shove, and for you to stand a little way off and watch. Then, you'll avoid being on a pedestal ready to be knocked off by another ego, as you're not in the competition of humanity at all.

The knack is to agree to lose. You don't have to play to win. Change your mind, agree to be last, and be happy with that. People might ask, "Aren't you bothered that you have to wait in line while other more important people go in front of you?" You'd reply, "No, it doesn't bother me. The people who need to strive, push, and fight to go first will burn themselves out and become sad. And while they may be in the front of today's line, tomorrow they won't have a place at all, and that may upset them. I'm happy to take any place in line—my position is irrelevant. I'm busy watching two sparrows talking on the roof over there."

Now here's an exciting notion that might impel you to another perspective. What if I told you that you could easily become one of the most powerful people in the world and have vast energy—so much that you could get almost anything you wanted just by deciding to materialize it? But there are a few strings attached: You can never tell anyone about it, and you can't do anything in front of people that might reveal your power to them—no performances, showing off, and so on. In fact, to make you keep to your agreement, you'll actually have to be anonymous about it all. Sometimes you'll purposely try to look like somewhat of a fool and incompetent, so people never catch on. I'm a bit handicapped for now because I write about it, but when I'm out and about and meet people, I never say anything—unless they ask me, that is.

Now here's another catch. You can have anything you want almost immediately. Materialize whatever you'd like, but since you possess the power, you'll never be able to use it because you're here to work, love, and understand the Earth plane. Your purpose is to transfer energy to others—that's it, the whole story. You can't use the power to become a tyrant or to enhance your ego to become the world's greatest something or other. You can keep bits of the energy to make your life easy and flowing, but you can't hoard the gift. You must get rid of it as it comes into your life; otherwise, you'd be misusing the power and bending it, just as many others have done.

The reason why the rule is in place is because the energy is so extreme and fast that it will fry you to madness if you try and hold on.

If you're serious about reaching the gap, you're saying that you'll work silently to arrive there and never tell a soul once you achieve it. Remember, enlightenment is the transmutation of your darkness; it's not spiritual elevation, concepts, or phantasmagorical things. Almost all of the initiates I know—the ones who have a real command of the hidden door (with the exception of one)—are humble and anonymous. You'd never spot them in a crowd; they don't have much to show . . . because they know.

You go beyond enlightenment because you don't need it; it's a trap for the spiritually naive. You probably knew that, but maybe you needed to be reminded. Perhaps the Hindus confused you. The fact is that the more inner power you have, the less you'll ever be able to show anyone. So then you may say, "Listen up, Stuie, bubba, what's the point of striving to acquire perception and abilities if I can't show anyone or make a profit from it all?" What's the answer? Here's what I learned, and it may be correct: All great power is always hidden so it can pass through the night and rescue people from the ivory towers of their tormented lives, loving and serving humanity to a better end. In saving people and flipping their minds, you'll have more than anyone else in the world, for you have the good karma of your noble deeds. You enter into bliss and radiate silently, and people will be endlessly pulled to you. It's an etheric thing within your life-force energy. You can help others without them ever knowing it.

There are celestial beings here. Maybe you don't see them right now, but they're here in the doorway, working tirelessly to retrieve this planet and humanity from the abyss. They're selfless and anonymous, and we strive to become like them. The beings I speak of are very real, and I know this is strange to say, but some will appear in the sky for everyone to witness. The images will be anywhere from 500 to 6,000 feet high, and they'll move and be alive and dynamic, hovering above us for days. Millions will see them. They're images in the Morph in the etheric of the world: Some will be angelic looking, and others will be historical figures or beings symbolic to a particular nation.

The reason I know that they'll be there is because I and others have already seen them—more than 20 apparitions in the sky so far. Each was easy to see. There were two over the parliament building in Budapest on the banks of the Danube: a man and a woman dressed as king and queen in ancient attire, holding a very large book. I found them very beautiful. Two of us saw them; they stayed in the sky all day until night fell. Eventually, they'll be there for the Hungarian people to see, and it will be inspiring. The apparitions in the sky are coming! It's hard to believe in the unseen, but I wouldn't tell you about them if I (and 18 others in five different countries) hadn't seen them already. I wouldn't mislead you. I write exactly and precisely what I see, allowing for the fact that when looking at transdimensional things, there's often more than one way of interpreting what one witnesses.

The Reversal of Misfortune

Let's go back to the reverse. The opposite of accu-mulation and egocentricity is humility, generosity, and service. Humbleness and the spirit of giving will bring you good fortune, but constant want and self-centeredness offer the prospect of a fall because it goes against the natural balance. At some point, you'll have to agree to serve, as you can't get out of this evolution and go beyond it without first doing so. At the end of your life, you'll see in retrospect that all the things you ever did for yourself count for very little. The great empires you won, the battles you fought, and all the striving will be the stuff of idle tattle.

There's only one currency of worth that you can take with you, and that's what you did and felt for humanity. Did you love and care for people? Did you go out of your way to make sure they were okay? Did you offer them what you had? Did you share or did you hoard? Did you run to eat first, or did you walk slowly and eat last?

Nothing else counts, for all the other ivory-tower stuff, empire building, and triumphs against other egos is all fluff. It shows how easily you can be tricked. All the anger and hatefulness is just one ivory tower clanging as it falls against others.

What have you done for others? That's the only question you'll be asked. If your karma is good, this will be easy. You'll humbly turn and wave your arms all around, and there will be those whom you healed, those whom you held when they were scared, those whom you provided for when they fell into misfortune, and so on. There might be thousands, tens of thousands, especially if you add in all the people you had a kind word for. It's unconditional love without having—or even expecting—to get something back in return.

Consider this: To incarnate successfully out of this physical evolution, you have to embrace humanity and grow to love us all—the good, the bad, and the ugly. You can only leave if you have a clean slate, meaning all things must be considered and resolved and forgiven, no matter what. So, unconditional love isn't just a squirt here and another there like cleaning fluid; it's the acceptance of everyone and everything. That's how you create the reversal of misfortune, which only came because you hadn't yet fallen in love with us all.

Once you let down your antagonism, the energy flips and the dark forces you insist on walking about with melt away to find another of the loveless. It's a necklace of skulls that you don't need. It's helpful to realize that all of life exists in a higher dimension, and while bits down here may be rather horrible, who are we to judge? At some deeper level, it must all make sense. To forgive and love is to set yourself free for divine things. Sometime in the next week or so, do something meaningful for some complete strangers without their knowing that you did it, and never mention it to them or anyone else. You'll soon understand the generosity of spirit that I'm speaking of.

There are people out there whom you haven't yet met, but they can't manage without you. They're like wounded children given the wrong set of coordinates— incorrect tumblers. Their life is bound to failure and misery, and what little meaning they have can be stripped from them in seconds. Their cells are becoming polluted by their darkness, and the slippery path to the end is in sight. They have no hope—none. They'll die surrounded by their ideals, ugliness, and dark forces. Only you can save them—if they want to come, that is. Your heart is the medevac tent of the MASH unit for those who were wounded in the great battles of the ego. That's your gift. Through it you'll reverse any misfortune you suffered in the past, and all that's lackluster will now become suitably enlivened.

There's a very special reason why this is true. We're all brothers and sisters, and we come from the same place. Remember Om and Ka? At a higher level, there's only one female and one male in the entire universe. Our separation is an illusion—we're not billions of different men and women. We're each inside an epic evolution, a digital, fractal formula that describes the vastness of the Celestial Man and Woman; you belong as an integer inside a complex blueprint. Imagine the entire universe as one person (Om), and inside that person is another being, which is light (Ka). These are evolving spirits like you and me. Earth is a spirit (Gaia), one cell rotating around inside that female body; and you're also a spirit who operates as a cell unit on the surface of that earth.

It's the same in that a cell in your kneecap isn't really a separate entity; it's a piece of a larger being—namely, you. To that cell you're God, the universe, and one day you'll evolve and become a universe yourself, or the light of one. But through egocentricity, you come to believe that you're the only man or woman, and that prevents you from achieving the greater whole. It keeps you from the light and strips you of your power base, forbidding your entry *(access denied)* into the greater mathematics of belonging to the immeasurable, celestial formula that describes the vast soul of the one man and woman. So, it cuts you off from vitality and information. When you assist others, it's no different from helping a cell in your body become more alive. It's obvious why people get sick.

Try this: As you walk down the street, breathe love into the hearts of your brothers and sisters. Do it to six people, and then rest and do six more. Make it a daily discipline, forever breathing adoration into people you don't know. At the same time, repeat to yourself: *Life is beautiful, people are beautiful* several times a day. Sometimes you can mentally place flowers in people's hearts as you pass them. Doing these things will change your resonance, for now you're a powerhouse of light and beauty, thinking about others rather than only about yourself. It's your offer of a celestial communion, one that also carries you from the tragedy of life as a single unit to your rightful place inside the vastness of everything.

As a part of delivering your soul to a spiritual redemption, you'll also guide others, and they'll become your tickets to the hidden doorway that I've mentioned. You become the gatekeeper for them like Merlin's friend, Nimue, who crossed back and forth for him. These individuals become your karmic passport through the portal by virtue of the very fact that you've rescued them. It's all in the feelings of your humanity, in the expression of it (how large and wide your heart can open), that you'll come to see the door to the transdimensional threshold lying within. But first, in order to get to this fantastic world, you have to travel across a dark and demonic world of discarnate entities and ghouls, remnants of the human shadow, while all manners of deviousness will try to stop you. Having a good resonance and perception of beauty helps you enormously, as it cloaks you in protection.

Enlightenment Transmutes the Dark

You have to learn to love the dark and not be afraid of it. Others taught you to fear it, but it was just a trick to make sure that you never made the journey. Edgar Cayce, the great American mystic, said that to get to his celestial worlds, he first had to go past the dark—that's correct. Two layers surround those realms: I call them the inner and outer matrix. (We'll discuss that in Chapter 5.) There's a beauty to the dark, as it's essentially the history of our collectively stored pain, and your anguish and the rest of the sorrow there is beautiful. It's how we all learned and transcended to become brave of spirit.

In time, you'll process that darkness within you, not by making it wrong or running away, but by loving and accepting it—then, nothing can touch you. Enlightenment is embracing the dark and transmuting it. In that maneuver, your evolution begins to turn the other way. It will power you along, and you need that flip of perception before you can access other things. I'll talk about the Morph and the mirror-world in the next chapters. I think you'll find it exciting and unusual, but first you must look and see if you have a genuine spirituality—a proper sweetness inside . . . or, do you just pretend to be nice?

Variance

In my book *Affirmations,* I talk about *variance;* bear with me while I briefly discuss it here, as the concept is valid in that it really talks about the essence of a positive reversal of self. Variance is the gap between what you pretend to be, what you think you are, the mask or persona you present to the world, and what you actually are. You could say that it's a tape, measuring the height of your ivory tower. All great spiritual journeys and the path of the initiate lead toward an ego death, a place where you become aware of the variance as the tower falls in front of your eyes. The authentic you has enormous power; when you join it, a synapse of energy occurs, which is a burst of light caused by a sudden fluctuation in the quantum field. This is vital to your enlightenment, for if you don't break down the illusion voluntarily, it's eventually collapsed for you. If you can control its demise over time, it's much less painful than when it crashes upon you in a fast hurry imposed from elsewhere.

Let me explain. People sometimes feel blank, hopeless, and despondent because they don't have the power of their own soul to drive them along. Their real identity is locked away, held prisoner in the tower. Have you ever felt that there was something terribly wrong or missing in your life? "You don't know what it is, but it's there, like a splinter in your mind," as the character Morpheus says in the first *Matrix* film. The lost bit is in the mirror-world. There's another you, the feeling you, and it's the one that's formed in the subconscious mind, holding the storehouse of your dreams. It's the authentic, perpetual memory of you—not your intellect and waking ideas, but your very soul. Once you come back and retrieve it, all sorts of creativity and possibilities arise from within. You have the opportunity to garner real worth in your life. Sure that imaginative insight might manifest as a nice moneymaking idea or just newfound friendships and a sense of belonging, but mainly it's a sense of well-being and abundance—not necessarily cash. It's the warmth of humanity, nature, and the animals around you; service to mankind and accepting help from others; and hope and serenity in a world of nasty ideas, madmen, and crazy women.

The emptiness you felt probably wasn't your fault; you might have been driven by fear and inadequacy, bad luck, or poor choices. We face many adverse factors. This isn't a level playing field, so you shouldn't be too harsh on yourself and others. Do this: Get a little notebook (one that you can slip into your purse or pocket), and over the next few days, jot down all the things in your life that make sense and the ones that don't. It's important to write them down, as it solidifies the concepts in your mind. Analyze your life: You're looking for the variance between what you have to do and how you really feel about it. Some of it will be obvious and you'll know that's it's phony, and some will be more obscure. It will only dawn on you as you think about it, asking your "superknowing" to show you. You must be fair and compassionate, and you can't cheat and lie to yourself, as that's a form of variance as well—isn't it?

Draw a line down the center of your booklet, and write *True* on one side of the line and *False, or Only Partly True* on the other side. Think about the following topics and questions:

— **Your job or business:** Do you like it? Are you content, or does it make you want to throw up?

— **Home:** Is the environment fulfilling and beneficial, or is it a bloody nightmare . . . like Elm Street? Is it where you want to be? Can you afford it?

— **Relationships:** Are they supportive or draining? Or, is romance killing you?

— **Money:** Are you sensible and honest or irrational and dishonest? Is the money thing always a dose of low-grade panic?

— **Lifestyle:** Is it healthy and sustaining or unhealthy and destructive? If it's harmful, it's probably your inner shadow trying to kill you. Are you brave enough to look at that and set yourself free, or will you remain a victim? Can you love yourself—lumps, bumps, and all? Will you save yourself in time?

— **Time management:** If you're rushing about with very little time for yourself, that's a variance of its own—one that you should examine. Remember, busyness is a death-avoidance mechanism for the neurotically challenged. The ego believes that *busy busy busy* makes you needed and important, and it serves as a distraction from the fear of death. As a tactic, this has a huge failure rate.

— **Caring:** Look and see if you really care about delivering your soul to a new redemption. Perhaps it doesn't really bother you or you feel that you're already perfect—such thoughts are a trap. Maybe you'll take your chances? I wouldn't if I were you. Via the Morph, I've been to those very dark inner worlds, such as the domain of the Lords of Cruelty; trust me, you won't like them. Sometimes I wish that every human could have at least one ten-minute look at those evil dimensions, and that would probably fix most of the world's problems. People would spook, and they'd soon vow to try a little harder on the opposite tack.

— **Tenderness:** Through awareness and perception, we enter the process of self-improvement. The key is to acknowledge how you relate to others. Are you distanced from humanity, or do you really care? Are you tender? Have you helped others? How much love do you offer, and how much of your thinking is silent resentment and hate? Are you an angel in disguise or a hidden predator? Are you stingy or generous? Are you open and accepting or closed down and dogmatic? Do you cast a kind eye toward everyone and offer a deep sense of justice and acceptance—live and let live—or are you judgmental and cruel?

— **Respect:** The way to work this out is to think about those whom you really don't agree with, and then ask yourself if you respect them anyway. Do you care for their humanity even if you don't like them? Do you feel compassion for their soul despite virulently disagreeing with their opinions and actions in life? This type of equanimity is vital because in the mirror-world, any kind of judgment or antagonism will soon take your spirit down. A lack of respect is a bad trait; you shouldn't denigrate others and make them wrong. You don't have to agree with everyone, but you eventually want your life to be seen as proper and right. How will you do that if you don't offer that same respect to others and you're always against them? Taking a truly equitable stance toward humanity and casting a kind eye is the only safe way to go across to the mirror-world.

— **Gratitude:** And finally, can I ask you a difficult question? Are you grateful? I mean are you truly appreciative, or do you just pretend? When you say thank you, do you mean it deeply from your heart, or is it just a social thing, fobbing people off? Are you actually relating to someone's soul and acknowledging them for their work or their kindness to you? I'm asking because I've noticed that people aren't grateful much of the time, and they don't bother to say thank you properly, if at all. They expect to be sustained, and they can't recognize the goodness that comes to them from others. Sometimes I think that they believe they're owed a living in this life regardless of how little effort they put in.

Gratitude is important; it goes hand in hand with humility and softness. It's part of respect—isn't it? Do you see how spooky and wonderful it gets real quick? If you do this right, it will make you cry because you'll see the darkness of it all. And if you only pretend to be thankful, or you have little real gratitude, you'll soon arrive back at *"access denied."*

When you see your callous lack of appreciation, it will become part of the torment of your shadow. You'll go through a crushing humiliation and utter despair, as the arrogance of the ego is thrown to the bonfire of your vanity, as Tom Wolfe might say. It's a terribly painful process but vital to your redemption. No one can save you from it, but once you see it and get to the other side, owning your lack of gratitude as one of your crimes against humanity and God, your life will dramatically change. I've seen many hundreds of people go through this process of self-realization; some of it was joy and other times it was tears and moments of heaving emotion, but in the end, they came out light and angelic and forgiven and liberated.

The greatest gift that you can offer yourself is redemption. Once you agree to stop running away, you'll be free and then you'll see it all properly. The destiny of humanity over the next ten years or so is to falter. People will be trapped, suckered into showing who and what they really are, and then again the fate of others will be to slip away, taking many with them. Some believe that Jesus will descend from the sky and redeem them. I can't say if that's right or not, but in all of the journeys that I've taken in the inner worlds and the hundreds that I've heard of, none has ever talked of a free ride. So, if you expect the Apocalypse and are waiting for Jesus, my advice would be to reform yourself in the meantime, just in case JC doesn't show up or if he does but misses you in the clamor and confusion of it all. I *dunno.*

I've never seen instant absolution or redemption. All there ever seems to be is a gradual climbing out from a hellish world of variance, confusion, and fake ideas toward a spiritually authentic world. Don't beat yourself up. It's okay to screw up—maybe that was your karma and others' as well. You just have to see and accept those aspects of who you are: the nice bits and the horrid ones.

Life can be scary and that may cause fear. The natural reaction is to become more aggressive, an increase in yang toward others, but eventual safety and a higher perception lie in the power of softness. Some know this already, but they don't always embrace it. It isn't obvious at first. The ego feels that the bigger threat it puts out, the more secure it will be, but that's not so. It isn't clear in the beginning, but the more aggressive you are, the greater the hard, devilish forces come against you because your energy is like theirs. So, spirituality is a measure of how tender and endearing you can become—not what rules you follow. It seems strange to go in the opposite direction, but in establishing a spiritual softness, you come to the first of three liberations.

The Three Liberations

Each of the three liberations is an emotional release and a spiritual advance, and it's best not to proceed without them. The energy of the world is rapidly shifting, and life could become increasingly challenging and problematical without these perceptions. You need energy-shifts to help you along.

The first liberation, as said, is that you have to agree to make peace with the world. What I've talked about so far is an unobtrusive attempt for you to resolve conflict with yourself, take to the reverse, and go the other way. This means that you must forgo the story of your life and evolve beyond that and all of its issues. That's the enlightened way. Your deliverance lies in processing the past, and this, of course, involves making peace with humanity. You can understand that if you're emotionally involved in running battles with others and you harbor resentments; you're perpetually linked to those people. It's as if you are spiritually welded to the individuals that you hate, fight with, or resent.

They may well have a terrible dose of low energy (and they may be abusers or predators and aggressive and/or arrogant), but you can't rise above them until you let them go. There's no percentage in being morally right; the only worth is in being free of them. In the mirror-world, which is a world of feelings, impulses, and sentiments, you can't escape from anyone that you're mentally or emotionally engaged with. It's a tag in the sense that they hold you in their locum, their energy spot. It's a place in the mirror-world (a geography) like I've mentioned before when talking about the Lords of Cruelty. Imagine it as a neighborhood. You can't fight with people while attempting to escape—they hold you. It's emotional glue.

Everyone has a story that involves pain, injustice, romantic upsets, and emotional hits that they've taken over the years, as well as the rip-offs and abuse suffered and all the times of hurt feelings. It's our special experience. You may feel very justified, and you may well have been an innocent victim, but you have to wonder in the overall karma of eternity. Are there really any innocent victims? If you believe in reincarnation, there might be a reason for your suffering, and it might explain why there seems to be so much injustice in the world. Sometimes people feel that they're blameless, but few things happen in a vacuum. If you knew all of the underlying feelings, you can see how we often taunt others emotionally in order for them to hurt us. It's ticking the testicles of a sleeping lion just to see if it will get pissed off and eat you.

The games we play when we feel injured are just a shadow process that we use to make ourselves holy and right. Or, we set ourselves up through greed to suffer a loss. But whether you were innocent, guilty, or even partly culpable, or if you brought misfortune upon yourself in some obscure way that you don't really understand, all that has to eventually become irrelevant as you now wish to proceed.

You've arrived in time for the "wrap and pack" show, but if you can't make peace with the world, you're stuck. The injustice you feel is part of the ancient stored pain that's inside of you; some of it exists because of the sins of the father or mother. It's suffering that's inherited through the centuries, unresolved clusters of dark energies trickling down through history. You'll never escape the global karma or your own while you're perpetually locked into the energy of your ex-husband or ex-wife, say, or people you've met on this journey through life. Let them go. You have to love your tormentors and offer them warmth and all the good will that you can muster (try not to vomit). An "eye for an eye, a tooth for a tooth" is a menu card for the reptiles' banquet, having no validity at all.

Beyond the people that you pulled to you in this life is the karma of your social or tribal cluster. A cluster is a grouping of people like a native tribe or even the members of the same golf club. So, the next liberation is the greater one of ditching what you were born with: the cluster that bound you. For example, if you were born an African American, you'll most likely have the injustice of slavery as part of your life's story. It will be in your genes, in your subconscious memory, and in the archetypes of your tribal heritage. And because of this, you may see the white man as a villain and tormentor, feeling threatened by him. He sits inside your shadow-self. You're the victim, and he's the slave trader. But wait a minute! Do any African-American slaves live in your hometown? Were you born a slave, or have you ever met one? Unless you're about 150 years old, you're bound to answer no.

So, if you're African American, you may have suffered discrimination (we all do in one form, or another), but the terrible injustice of slavery isn't really part of this life; it's just a rotten story from the past. The problem is in having white men in your shadow as the enemy: You push away all the white men and women who might help you in this life, those who might give you a hand up. Do you see how the tribal shadow is so destructive and how it holds you back? It's the same for the Jews. They have their sad stories; and the Palestinians' story says how dark and nasty the Jews are, and so they're inside the Palestinian shadow, as the Germans are inside the Jewish shadow and so forth. Each is trapped by the other, but all that terribleness is usually in the past. You have to let it go.

Become spiritually mature and grant yourself the second liberation, the one that allows you to go beyond your religious, social, tribal, or national karma. You don't need it anymore, for you want to arrive at a place where you see yourself as an eternal being—loving, evolving, and spiritual—not an African; a Jew; a poor, downtrodden Catholic in South America; a disenfranchised woman; a wounded Muslim in the Middle East; and so on. It's all "story," nothing more—and in the dimension of the celestial, it doesn't really exist. For in there, all darkness is transmuted into light and strength.

Some of the story probably isn't even true, but it serves a purpose while you're still unsophisticated. For those who haven't resolved their shadow-self "need" their special story. They need the memory of pain suffered so they can now feel squeaky clean, holy, and right. And sometimes they use that to garner money and compensation, sympathy, an advantage as a victim, or some special status in their family or tribal cluster. It's a way for everyone to be very angry all of the time. Often your sense of injustice is an illusion linked to a form of self-importance that's usually hidden inside your subconscious mind. It's how you make yourself more holy and good, but it's deadly for progress. For you to spiritually step to another world, you must be finished with the ugly emotions of this one.

I don't mean that you have to die, but you need to resolve the pain, understanding it in the light of your shadow, and how that hidden power source pulled events to you. Then you see it all in a grand scale, stop complaining, and go past it. If not, you'll die spiritually weak, floundering in the cluster of the anguish of your tribe. You'll drift to that part of the mirror-world where the wounded Jews are sitting next to the wounded Muslims; and they're close to all the Native people, who deeply suffered under the white invaders. And over here is a group of four million tortured Irish souls, people who died in the famine; they have the English in their shadow. Soon you can see how our human evolution is knotted and interlaced, a neck scarf of misery tied 'round the throat of our humanity: my pain, yours—the collective Jungian pain. If you can't go beyond it, you're stuck. You'll float down the pain drain. Where does that lead? Nowhere.

I know that it's hard to go past a sense of injustice and the rage that certain political and social issues evoke. I spent 20 years on my high horse picking nits out of my ears, indignant about all sorts of things, but I eventually got two things through my thick head. First, the greatest injustice was that I wasn't fair to myself; the second realization was that we didn't incarnate into a world that's fair—so get over it. We didn't come to a planet where people are respectful and caring of each other, nature, animals, or the environment. So, the only option is believing in a higher order that we can aspire to, and that higher beings watch over us to protect things and won't allow Earth to fall into absolute degradation and destruction.

That brings us to the third liberation: the ability to see that injustice is part of our global karma—it's part of the planet's karma, the animal's karma, and so forth. We have to hold steady in the face of injustice, knowing that there must be a fair resolution eventually, even if we haven't much evidence of it so far. All experiences exist at a higher level because we exist there. In the end, all injustice will be set right and all sadness will melt away—maybe not in our lifetime, but later. Then again, we might be in for a wonderful surprise. There's a group of beings from another world who have recently found their way into this dimension (see page 173) and right now we're waiting to see how their presence will affect things . . . all isn't lost!

So, the first liberation is when you allow all those who have hurt you to go on their way. Good riddance to bad rubbish. And through the second liberation, you release any social or tribal clusters that trap you. The final liberation is that you go beyond the anger and pain of the terrible injustices suffered by the planet as an organism, the animals, and the general tragedies that people endure every day. If you're sensitive, the pain of the world will probably bother you to no end. But right now, there isn't much that we can do, as political systems are stacked against us; and there are so many billions of people living in abject poverty, loneliness, and despair.

You have to have compassion for the suffering of humanity and dedicate yourself to helping those you come across. But it also serves us to see that we're power-less for now, as it's one of our spiritual lessons. We must first become humane, and then we're given the ability to change. We liberate ourselves from that sense of helpless-ness, not by buying a gun, but through love and gentle-ness; and we offer the greater responsibility, or most of it anyway, to higher beings in the hope that they have the power and knowledge we lack.

We don't know why there has to be so much anguish, although it has a lot to do with the evil in our collective human shadow. All you can do is process your darkness and redeem it. Don't let yourself be overwhelmed by the global situation. And if you say to me, "But Stuie, I'm a one-eyed, Chinese gay male with a wooden leg, and I have loads of emotion and pain; and in my cluster, there's Tiananmen Square, the Long March, and the millions who perished in the Cultural Revolution. I can't do 'bye-bye, Beijing' right now! I need to clunk around here for a bit longer and work it all out" . . . I'd respond, "Sure, bro', come when you want—there's no rush."

Let's go to the next chapter, and I'll talk about the rescue that's here. It's the one that we've seen in the phenomenon of the Morph, and I'll show you how to get there, which may give you a sight of yourself in the mirror-world, propelling you past sticky cling-wrap clusters to a higher plane. Hanging around at this old level will tire you out. Onward!

CHAPTER THREE

THE MYSTERY OF THE MORPH, GRACE, AND YOUR MIRROR-SELF

The Morph phenomenon is at the doorway of a multi-dimensional hyperspace, surrounding the gate of the Grail castle. It's everywhere. Viewing it is nothing more than trusting that it's there, deciding that you want to see it, and understanding that you will if you desire to. It's best to try it when you're a little bit tired—at the end of the working day, say, because that's when your brain cells oscillate at slower speeds. It's in the lower wave band called theta, which is four to seven cycles per second, where it all becomes clear.

Seeing the Morph

Sit in a room with the lights off (or you can lie on your bed if you like), and focus on the idea that you'd like to witness the Morph, knowing that it's everywhere, so it must be around you right now. It's a flip of the mind to decide to become wider, less linear, and you agree to believe in the unbelievable. Be sure that the room is almost completely dark, but leave just enough light through a crack in the door—enough for you to be able to make out your hand when it's outstretched two or three feet in front of your face. Now, stare at the far wall or the ceiling, and then bring your concentration back to the halfway point: the midair between you and the wall or ceiling. That's where the Morph is hovering. If you try too hard or strain, it somehow spoils the process. You have to see without looking, relaxing your eyes. It's much like those images that have holograms hidden within. The more you push your concentration forward, the less you see. But if you relax and pull your concentration back, the invisible picture suddenly pops into view.

The Morph is similar: When you realize how to look, your mind "clicks" to it every time. It's so alive that you really can't miss it once you've seen it. It's full of swirls and sparkling lights that look like tiny glowworms; we call the twinkling lights "the speckled ambience." The sight of it evokes a sense of bliss that seems to call to you from some mysterious part of your inner self.

It's the grace of the eternity that we all belong to that's manifested into something tangible. In the Morph, you'll also see fast-moving diagonal lines crossing the room, which look like dry rain. Sometimes you might view flashes like mini–lightning bolts; in other instances, you'll see visions appear in your mind's eye or watch video clips play as if projected on the wall. They can fry your noodle big time, as you keep wondering where on earth they're coming from!

The first Morph "video" that I ever saw was a 45-minute movie of a cat fighting with dark animals in a forest. The clip started playing spontaneously on a wall, as if a TV screen had been switched on. It was in black and white, but gradually, the images became lightly dusted in various colors. As the film played, I felt a strange tugging sensation on my navel that made me feel queasy. There were graphic scenes where the cat would rise up and fight with another animal, both hovering a few feet off the ground. The cat won every battle except the last, and after each one, it sat on the ground grooming itself.

Then, the camera went up the trunk of a tall fir tree, and at the top I heard a voice say, "Look at the stars." It was cloudy above the forest, and there wasn't anything to see. Thirty-nine times the camera followed the tree trunk upward, and each time I heard the same instruction to look at the stars that weren't there. Obviously, this was a significant message. I think it was saying to observe how the dark forces have clouded humanity's view of the heavens.

All this happened during the day, in the front room of a suburban home near London. The film started up on the wall without a projector, DVD, or VCR—*nothing*. I found it hard to understand, but it came out of the Morph. As it played, I got very tired, and the tugging at my navel became so intense that I started to hope the film would stop, which it eventually did with one last fight: the cat versus a fox.

They fought in midair—it was a fantastic battle. The cat wasn't the victor this time; it was a stalemate between the two of them, as the fox turned and walked out of the area. I think the lesson is that we can never overcome all of the dark, only parts of it. After the fox left, humans arrived. They looked ordinary; many were dressed in jeans and T-shirts. They looked around in wonderment, and the message I got from that was that the cat had cleared the forest so that it would be a safe place for the humans to live—the cat created a Camelot and offered it to others.

Many people I know have seen the video clips from the Morph, like the cat film. Some are short—under a minute. And I saw one that was just ten seconds long, but it repeated over and over for three to four hours. Appearing in the green color of night-vision glasses, it was a video of the death of Diana, the princess of Wales. It shows the black car entering the Alma tunnel in Paris; then there's an explosion under the front wheel on the driver's side, and the car hits a pillar and spins around. I observed the video carefully, and once it stopped, there was a slight pause and then it replayed. If, say, it played four times a minute over a period of three or four hours, I would've watched it between 720 and 960 times. With that clip came ten more that played out of the Morph over the next few months. They showed the whole assassination in fine detail: how the car (which had been stolen some weeks before) was switched and set up in France. What it didn't reveal was *whodunit!* We'll have to wait for that story to come out, as it remains a mystery.

The Morph is all around you; call for it, and it will come and show you. You'll soon realize that you're much further ahead than you believe yourself to be. You may have known for a while now that something is going on with the metaphysical reality of this world, but maybe you haven't had the right terms with which to explain it. Sometimes the Morph will be stronger than at other times, but it never leaves. So, many of you have already experienced it without ever knowing. Now let me say this: The sight of the Morph isn't something reserved for high adepts, Hindu holy men, or great spiritual leaders—the purple Poo-Bah of the Seventh Ray and all that malarkey. It's for everyone, and thousands of people have already seen the Morph; and some—like you—will learn to use it. It's the grace of the feminine spirit here to heal the soul of the world. It has to be common and for everyone—that's obvious.

The Disappearing Hand

Another way to view the Morph is to raise your arm in the air in a darkened room and focus on your fingertips. See if you notice flashes of energy coming off the ends. The Morph takes oxygen out of the air, and it never comes down lower than about two to three feet from your face. It knows where you are in the room, which is why you have to raise your arm above yourself. You may see your index finger morphing off to the right at an angle of 45 degrees. Then if you watch carefully, you'll first see your fingers shortening and gradually (if the Morph is strong that day), your hand will disappear completely. This is very common; it happens every time the Morph comes into a room. I've witnessed it more than 500 times, maybe even a thousand times.

The "C" Vortex

Here's another way, but it's a little harder to see, depending on how good your perception is. If you cup your hand and make a C shape with your forefinger and thumb, you'll discover a small tube of morph-light between the bottom of your finger and top of your thumb. That little tube is about the thickness of a cigarette: It's a minivortex. As I was writing this bit, I took a break to have a drink with a couple of friends in a cocktail bar, and I showed them the C vortex. The lighting in the room was subdued, and the front of the bar was black marble; in these conditions, they both saw it easily.

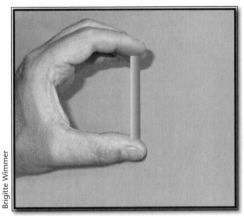

Brigitte Wimmer

The Morph tube between the fingers.

If you can see the C vortex in one hand, then try to view it with the other at the same time. Now rotate one hand through 90 degrees and push it in toward the other one so that the two vortices intersect and make a cross, much like a plus sign (+). When they overlap, you'll feel a faint tingle as they interfere with each other.

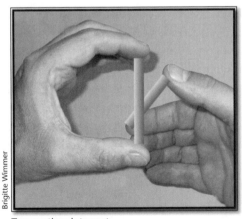

Brigitte Wimmer

Two vortices intersect.

Now if you touch both of your thumbs together and both forefingers at the tips, they'll form a triangle. In its center, there's another vortex. It's a gateway to another world, albeit a very small one.

Brigitte Wimmer

The location of the vortex between your fingers.

Have someone slowly put their index finger through the center of the triangle; he or she should be able to feel a slight downward, tugging sensation, like the pull we experienced when the upside-down Y appeared over the bed at my house in Milton. If you look carefully, you'll see the finger elongate as it enters the vortex in the center of the triangle formed by your fingers. Their finger begins to morph between the first knuckle and the tip, as the vortex in your hands pull it down. As you see the finger stretch, it partially disappears, and the individual will feel the slight heat of it and a light tingling sensation.

Both my pals in the bar saw the elongation easily the first time they tried it. Remember that the lighting has to be subdued and the background dark, like the black marble in the bar. If you can see either the C vortex or the one in the center of the triangle, you'll understand that the hidden door of the Holy Grail that I spoke of isn't far away or impossible to find. I told you that it wasn't hard—not as difficult as people think.

It's extraordinary to comprehend that the Grail doorway is in your hands. So, the traveling aspect of the Grail quest is pointless, for you have the door with you the entire way. Funny, eh? The Morph revealed the C vortex to me early on. We're being led by the hand, like little children being taken two by two across a lawn through a pretty garden. The journey isn't very long, and it's safe—trust me. I'm here to tell the tale . . . I found that rather encouraging.

This Morph thing is alive and all around us, renewing and reviving our bodies. Sometimes you can see it and sometimes you can't. One day my left hand started to prickle like crazy, and I watched over a period of 20 minutes while my skin cells rejuvenated. The brown spots, pimples, and faint blotches disappeared; and the skin became creamy looking, as if my hand had gone back 30 years in time. The gift of the Morph will become a great power in this world. When it showed me the rejuvenation of my left hand, the same process didn't happen on my right one, and I could clearly see the difference between the two once it was over. In case you're wondering, it may have already begun the healing process on you, as so many people have experienced the Morph without realizing it.

The Eye Twitch

With the Morph comes various bodily sensations. The most common begins with a twitching of the eyes that can last a few days or even weeks. When I experienced this, it worried me at first, and I wondered what was wrong, not knowing that it was caused by the Morph. Then one day the twitching stopped. I never discovered what it meant, but it marked the beginning for me.

The Download Buzz

Then, there's what we call *the buzz*. It's a low-volume, high-pitched buzzing, like a whine that seems to move around inside your head. Often you imagine that it's behind you, as if it's hovering three or four inches from the back of your skull around the base of the cranium. Sometimes you'll hear it move from one side of your head to another, like when you pan the speakers' direction on a stereo system, hearing that whoosh of the music going from side to side. The buzz can be quiet, soft, and gentle; and then at other times, it becomes louder. Some days it's not there at all. It ebbs and flows—you'll get used to it. If you have the buzz, it's a gift—a grace develops from it over time. It's energy and information coming from another world, a transdimensional download so you oscillate faster. The shamans of South America call the buzz the "airplane" because to them it resembles the rumbling sound of planes passing overhead.

Now there's a type of ringing in your ears called tinnitus, but that's very different from the buzz. Tinnitus is a medical condition in which a ringing is clearly heard in one or both ears, while the buzz is more spatially located and constantly moves. At times the buzz is less electric and loud, and it changes to become a soft shushing sound, like white noise (which as you may know, is the quiet noise that you hear from electronic equipment when it's turned on but not engaged in playing). When it shifts to white noise, it's usually accompanied by a sense of bliss that may last many hours or even days.

There's another audio sensation that I call *formatting,* which you may have already heard. It's a faint tick-tick sound that seems to be limited to one ear. (I can hear it now as I'm writing this.) It reminds me of the noise that computer floppy disks made in the olden days when you had to format them before use. I don't totally know what the sound represents yet, but again, it's another download. In one vision, I saw that it's part of the construction of a dome-shaped cage that looks like it's made of strips of red neon light. It's protection of some kind. I do know what formatting looks like, as I've seen it, coming down the side of a funnel like a megaphone. Here are diagrams that illustrate the whine/buzz wave pattern and the formatting sound moving down the cone.

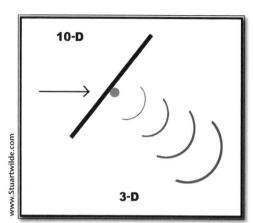

Whine/buzz wave pattern transmitting via the Morph to our 3-D world.

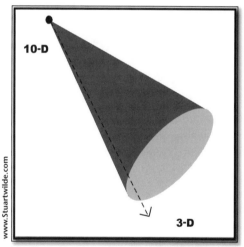

The formatting sound comes down a cone.

Sometimes you'll also hear a soft clicking that seems like the light tapping of drumsticks. This is usually due to anomalies or fluctuations in the electromagnetic field around you. It's heard a lot in poltergeist cases, which may not be the actions of evil spirits but the warping of reality in places where strong electromagnetic fields cross, like in a valley where there are phone towers on the surrounding hills.

The Flutter

You may have also experienced what we call the *flutter*. It's the sensation that your nervous system seems to be slightly fluttering. In men, it often starts between the lower legs at the ankles, and women seem to first experience it in the chest area. I remember in the early days telling a doctor about the flutter, and he looked at me blankly; he had no idea what I was talking about. I've known people who became really scared thinking that they had Parkinson's disease, but the flutter isn't an ailment. It's very similar to the prickling I felt on my hand. It's a wonderful gift if you get the flutter, as it will boost your system, and your cells will begin to rebuild themselves as they take to a higher vibrancy. We noticed that people who've experienced the flutter over a period of years look bright and lucent, often beginning to look more youthful as time goes by.

There are about 50 sensations of the Morph, so I can't deal with them all here. One includes a neck flip that occurs at night while you sleep; it's a series of electric shocks in various parts of the body whereby your muscles twitch and release energy. Sometimes the twitches are so strong they almost knock you off the bed. These *elecs*, as I call them, are big inputs of energy coming in from another world. At times, you may feel the shocks right in the center of your heart, making it feel like it's flipping over. Don't worry, as they provide healing and won't harm you. One of my pals says that to him, it feels like there's a little squirrel tumbling 'round in his chest. The elecs can come in bunches—one after the next. It can be a bit disturbing, as you don't know when they'll stop. My record is 64 shocks that occurred every three minutes for approximately three hours. That was hard work!

Sometimes you'll see small circles with dots in them, crossing your field of vision. If the circle is going from left to right, say, it means that your etheric is moving in the opposite direction. If it's drifting downward, then your energy is traveling upward. You're always going in the opposite direction to the motion of the circle. At times, you'll also see little sparkles of colors, usually blue, silver, yellow, or red. And you may see what looks like little silver worms—thin ones, squiggling in front of you. These are all Morph features. I find that the Morph is full of grace and mystery, yet some of it is slightly weird because it's a world in which we know very little about.

If at first you don't see the Morph, don't worry. It could be because of two things. The first is that some people are very cerebral, meaning that they're great thinkers. They're not used to a world of subtle feelings; and they don't believe much, if at all, in the unseen. Often these people don't have any visions or dreams whatsoever. They're the computer programmers of this world, living in the domain of intellectual ideas. Everything must follow logic, or they feel exposed, unsafe, and open to ridicule. If you're like that, give yourself time. You need to trust and let go. Your mind may be very bright, which is an asset, but it will never achieve a place of enlightenment or beyond, for the transdimensional world doesn't follow anything that we can understand. The strange anomaly found in quantum physics—where a particle suddenly appears and disappears—tells you what to expect.

There's nothing wrong with the intellect, but it eventually runs out of steam. There are only more and more questions. Sometimes bright people—like university professors, for example—have such powerful minds that their thoughts gradually become godlike to them, in that thinking becomes their religion. If you're like that, your life will be frustrating, for the only way that humans can evolve beyond the mind is to enter into the supernatural, and that world isn't logical.

There are dimensions that hover in a type of inner hyperspace, where you can't tell what's up or down, inside or out, and so on. It's all very fleeting, and perception as you know it is subtle. Some people are a bit coarse and cynical, so they're higher perception is minimal. Life becomes fearful because they have difficulty seeing the future. They have to guess, and they don't believe that there's a grace or flow of divine light coming into their life.

The second reason for not being able to see the Morph is that a long time ago you forgot how to look. I don't mean to be glib here—the forgetting is often a fact. When you were a child, you could see the gap, but later you simply couldn't remember how to do it. It slipped from your mind because you became busy with schoolwork and the lessons of life.

Start to look for what isn't there. For example, gaze into the space between things, and see if you can make out the subtle striations caused by interference patterns. Here's an exercise that shows you what this looks like: Put your forefinger and middle finger together, and bring them up to the height of your eyes, holding them ever so slightly apart. In the small space between your fingers, you'll see little black lines. This occurs because photons of light interfere with each other in order to pass through the small gap. If you can't observe it immediately, make the opening a bit bigger or smaller—adjust as needed. Don't do it in a brightly lit area; find a spot where the light is more diffused. The Morph and the human etheric are both interference patterns, caused when one source of light crosses another, enabling us to see them.

There's a sensation that I call *fat time:* when your sense of time goes very long and wide. If you know the feeling, then you've seen the edge of the gap because a time anomaly exists there. The more you can slow down your perception, the closer you are to the gap and rushing about too much takes you further away from it. If you can learn to drag time back toward you, you'll then approach the Grail door.

We can practice this by trying to visually stop a revolving ceiling fan. Normally when it's full on, it's spinning too fast to observe the individual blades, but if you can momentarily pause time with your mind, you'll see a single blade as if it's frozen. You're now watching the suspended animation of the eternal; in effect, it's a stutter in the forward motion of time. The still image you see is historically behind where the blade actually is in the present, so you're looking at it backward in time.

The fan trick is hard to do, but it eventually comes from looking at patterns that appear between reality—the spaces around the leaves of a tree, and so forth. Also, start to listen to people when they're not talking and see what you perceive in their feelings, their silent talking. Most of a conversation is the result of the speaker's inner impulses that convey information. Try to discover what's hidden behind that impulse. Be humble and pray that you'll remember how to do this. (If you're interested in learning about silent talking, I wrote a book about it called *Silent Power*, which was published by Hay House.)

Maybe all that you need is a bit of an energy lift, especially if you feel flat and ill at ease. You may be used to looking for energy to sustain you from outside sources (such as food, drugs, alcohol, or sex), or it's gone stale from incessantly watching TV. Perhaps your entire life you've sought things that would create momentary bursts of pleasure, and you've never thought to sit very still in a dark room and wait and trust. Excitement is okay, but perception is better, as it has real value and brings its own thrills.

You should keep a journal where you write down any dreams, visions, or unusual sensations. I take a small handheld recorder with me. At times you'll be walking along and something will trigger a big realization. You should jot that down, as bit by bit it will form a pattern. It's your higher knowing from an inner world talking to you, communicating in symbols that are different to each of us, so it has to accumulate a vocabulary that your waking intellect will learn and understand. These are early days, and you have to allow the process to unfold. Nothing like this has ever happened in the history of psychic powers, metaphysical happenings, and spiritual events. So, it could take a while, as nature goes much slower than we do.

If you have an intellectual cynicism that prohibits you from believing in ephemeral things and the unseen, it's a hindrance because what you can see and prove is very small—even the entire universe is minute compared to inner space and the other dimensions. If you're keen but can't get past your skepticism, just pray that the powers that be grant you one extraordinary experience that will blow away the walls of logic. You must be humble about it (and some might have to put aside that irritating habit of pretending they know everything), for if your mind is unwieldy, the higher powers can't really show you. You have to be allowed to believe whatever you want—that's the law, someplace. But you'll get your special moment if you pray for it.

Remember, we humans are programmed to forget and to be etherically and transdimensionally blind. You have to have faith without any evidence, and then eventually, it will open up a little and show you. But you must go first.

Do this for a while: Agree to believe in everything. Buy those funny mags at the supermarket that say "Three-headed werewolf buys suburban home in Maryland!" It's silly, but just try to take it as fact in order to practice believing. It won't hurt you, and you'll become less stiff. In this way, you gradually pull the invisible into your life so things build upon one another. (Many mystics and holy people and the Hopi Indians have predicted a new age of enlightenment, and they're not wrong in my view. It has arrived, and with it comes a whole host of fascinating phenomena never before seen. We're stepping into a magical new era: the age of forgiveness.)

The Master Plan

The trick is to embark on a plan to raise your energy, making yourself more aware of the gap. If your energy is increased, you'll feel secure, less scared, and able to perceive in greater depth. There's a mass of information in the digital, fractal data banks of the inner worlds that will talk to you incessantly once you click in. If at first you can't see, then you might have to create a threshold experience for yourself. For example, as part of a master plan, set aside a few days when you're off work, and go out on your own, silently and in nature—up in the mountains, say. You might need to pull away from the stress and worry of life and day-to-day circumstances, for those can warp your image of self and corrupt your perception of life. Sometimes we lose connection with spirit and the sacred nature of who we really are and what this life is about. The threshold experience often gives you the first act of remembering—recalling your true self.

A simple example of this would be if you've sadly allowed your life to become repetitive and boring, hardly ever having time off. Soon, your mind comes to believe that nothing unusual could ever happen and that life is always flat and monotonous. What you believe is what you see, and it's also what you get. My friend Wayne Dyer wrote a book called *You'll See It When You Believe It*—a clever title because it's so right. Dullness and a lack of imagination hold you back. Sometimes you can't evaluate what's under your nose. Relationships that are loving will always sustain you, yet sometimes they're so scary and toxic that they cloud your mind. You don't notice that they're killing you, as you've become a blind slave to the ideals of another and to what you think they want from you.

By getting away, you rediscover yourself. You get to turn within, see what light you do have, and learn to guard it better. I take time out on my own quite regularly, sometimes going on the road for months at a time. It's vital to me. Yes, it can be a lonely journey, but in the quietness or when walking in nature, I'm beyond the boundaries of my life, and I see things that I didn't before. Deepak Chopra told me that he goes away for nine days on his own a couple of times a year. Sometimes you need the isolation.

I also fast from time to time as a way of bringing my energy up. I'll go without food for just three days, and other times I'll do it for five to nine days. Now, if you have low-blood-pressure problems or other health concerns like diabetes, you shouldn't try this without discussing it with your health-care professional. There's a small percentage of people who don't do well with fasting, yet many others can benefit greatly from it, as it opens a soft doorway inside you. Your energy becomes more rarified, and you become gentle and aware of unseen things.

A threshold experience—like three days of fasting in silence on your own—can carry you from coarse and asleep to awake and alert. Then, suddenly you'll view the Morph, even though you were looking at it the entire time but couldn't see it. It's there, and the Morph acts as a lens for you to peer into other worlds.

Ascension Goes Sideways

Here's a flip you have to make: People think that a higher vibration is upward, but energy that's moving faster isn't really going up. It's going sideways. If you're one who knows of the other worlds and have already fallen off the roof of the tower, you'll know that it's the key. "Sideways?" you might ask. Yep. Sideways will become part of your plan. The ego living on the tower believes that "up" must be the right way—higher and higher, more and more. The fool on the top is attracted to height, but sideways is the correct way. And it took the Morph to reveal that to us.

Jesus might have ascended into heaven after the crucifixion; I can't say if that's true or not. Christians have to accept it on faith. But I can tell you this: If Jesus did ascend into heaven, he didn't go up because there's nowhere to go. If you head straight up, you'll soon have altitude problems and your lungs will collapse. If he went anywhere, it was sideways. He ascended sideways and dematerialized! That's because the doorway to the spiritual heaven that we all seek is at 90 degrees, about three to four feet away from us. We're in a bowl: If you spin around, the door is always off the end of your outstretched fingertips.

The Sideways Motion of Light

"When in doubt, baffle 'em with science," so they say. Here goes: Light travels in a straight line at about 300,000 kilometers per second. But what people don't usually realize is that it also has a motion at 90 degrees to the straight line. There's a zigzag, sideways movement to light as well as the forward one. It's described in a branch of mathematics called *imaginary numbers*. If you want to dematerialize and enter into a heavenly dimension, you'll learn to etherically slide across sideways.

You can trust me on that for two reasons: First, everyone who's ever tried to make it by going up failed miserably; and second, the sideways motion is the only way that you can ever go backward in time because it's faster than light. Now, it's not your physical body that would travel at this speed, but your etheric one—your life force. To evolve beyond this tick-tock world, you have to think out of the box and fold back on yourself into that sideways world.

Let me explain. Einstein's laws of light refer to the forward motion of light in a vacuum, but the sideways momentum isn't very fast at all. In fact, the waves swing back and forth at 4,000 to 8,000 pulses a second. So, you have to imagine thousands of zigzag lines crossing the main light beam every second.

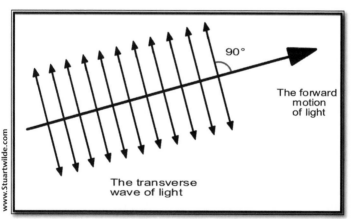

90°

The forward
motion
of light

www.Stuartwilde.com

The transverse
wave of light

The sideways motion of light.

If your life force (the etheric) oscillates sideways at over 8,000 cycles a second, you'll actually be going faster than light. You escape from the valley between the crests of the waves, and you have 1/8,001th part of a second to slip away. It sounds unlikely, but the etheric knows how to do it. It can move even faster than that. This was one of half a dozen things that we were first taught in the Morph. We were shown the diagram that I've included here. It's quirky to think of the old Taoist writers who said, "The Valley Spirit never dies." They were far ahead of their time, as what they wrote is technologically correct. You escape to eternity from the valley between the transverse waves (as illustrated in the diagram).

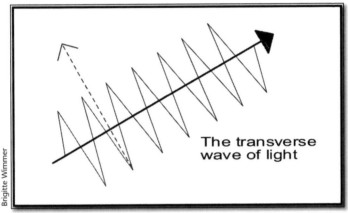

The valley between waves of light.

Nothing physical, like a human, can move forward faster than light. If you were to approach its speed, you'd get heavier and heavier, and it would take an infinite amount of energy to accelerate you over the threshold. But the notion that the human etheric can move side-ways *faster* than light has now been proven in the Morph over and over. The sideways motion will grant you a perception of the future because you enter a world where past, present, and future exist simultaneously. You need that wide view for your master plan, as it will help you understand the karma of people and nations and make critical decisions at exactly the right time. So, you hop from one lily pad to another when needed—don't worry, it's easy. You've done it before, haven't you? It's all in the art of remembering . . . again.

When you lie down to meditate (or if you do it sitting in a chair), first imagine yourself sliding off to the left, say. It's just a creative visualization, and even if in the beginning, you can't get your etheric to cooperate, you can make it happen over time by imagining, as the etheric always follows your vision in the end. It's as if your soul knows what direction it wishes to proceed in. You might also try this when lying down during meditation: See if you can rotate your energy so your head is at your feet, and your feet are where you head is. That 180-degree flip is the gateway to another mirror-world. In relation to it, humans are upside down and inside out, just like the display of those old-fashioned telescopes. That's why it's said that humans are inside out. That part comes from the fact that the inner you is the genuine one, and this body and life aren't as real.

Do you see how interesting this system is? The tower is all up, which requires more and more gratification, illusion, electricity; and all the stress, futility, and struggle to sustain self-importance. But once it collapses, the ego is tamed and sometimes humbled. It's allowed to rest at last. Once it consolidates—and if you hurtle through the three liberations that we spoke of earlier—your energy will automatically shuffle off sideways, toward the dimension of transverse light because there's nothing else holding it back. It goes naturally from a cold existence of isolation on the windy tower to a warm one with other people; animals; the healing of the planet; and all of the natural domains of softness, love, compassion, and acceptance.

Sideways eventually takes you to one certainty: that you never really had a clue. In fact, as you grow more and become truly transdimensional, you'll realize that you don't know very much at all—none of us do. All I'm telling you here is how to arrive at the 90-degree nowhere land. I can't begin to describe the fractal celestial worlds past the door where the higher beings exist. They're from beyond the great vastness. At the end of this journey and if you transcend, there's just the eternal void; and in the spiritual purity of it, there's nothing and everything. All is wiped clean. In the empty expanse, what point of reference would you use to decide if you're up or down, illuminated or not? And looking back from that void, it all looks silly. *Enlightenment* is just a term invented by spiritual people to trap the ego. I don't think you need it—it's far too heavy.

Make it a part of your plan to get rid of one aspect of the ivory tower every week, drifting toward simplicity and redemption. Today you sell the second car; next week, you donate some of the designer clothes; and after that, you liberate yourself from someone who's trouble or in the way, releasing them emotionally. Then, get rid of a bad habit, lovingly settle an argument with someone, sell some more of your accumulated rubbish and use the money to settle a debt, and so forth.

I did an inventory of people in my life, and you might want to do the same as part of your threshold plan. Write down the names of all the people whom you know and deal with—the ones who impact your life: family, friends, and business associates, for example. Then, sit quietly and bring them up in your mind's eye. How many really love and support you, accepting you unconditionally? Who is a waste of time or feeds off of you emotionally, draining energy or money? How many of them are honest or dead dodgy? Who lies to you?

I've always found that if a person lies about a small thing, he or she will eventually lie about big things. And when you come upon people who deal in deception, whatever energy you express in their direction will eventually bring tears and heartache. Lying is vertical, and embracing the truth is a sideways move. Catch yourself every time you exaggerate or bend the facts and in any instance when you deliberately give someone an erroneous impression, offering faulty information. Learn to become scrupulously honest! Make a point of noticing when you're in denial, glossing over events, or interpreting them in a dodgy way to suit your story. Try to be truthful with yourself, and agree to live like that as much as possible—remembering, of course, that none of us is perfect.

The reason for all this effort is because over in the mirror-world, the alternative you is made up of your subconscious memories, feelings, and impulses; and it seeks to operate authentically. Naturally, it cringes each time you go the other way, are dishonest or covert, or when you act outside of what's proper and correct. Your mirror-self constantly prompts you in your dreams by firing through subtle feelings. It's trying to explain things, hoping that you go toward what's healthy, truthful, and beneficial, and steer clear of all that's phony and dark. Remember that you're always being watched, not just by demonic entities who lurk close by, waiting for a resonance to latch on to, but by angelic beings, ready to help you when needed. They're also curious to see which way you go in any given situation. And then you have your mirror-self, who's also observing, in the sense that it's collecting a record of every feeling you express in your life. Nothing is ever lost.

I'll conclude with this: Your waking intellect makes decisions and choices, and it impels you to speak and act from its desires. And from those words and actions come consequences—some pleasing, some not so pleasing. In the process of operating your life with your intellect, you generate feelings that you may not be immediately aware of. Those sentiments are stored in the mirror-self, which is your eternal, spiritual identity. So, it's not so much what happened in this life; it's more how you felt about what did happen and how your actions affected others. In other words, your whole life comes down to a memory of feelings.

The Memories of Trees

I've always been attracted to the mysticism of the Celts and spent a lot of time in the forest in Ireland with local scalawags and shaman types. The Celts grant nature a resonance and a feeling, believing that trees have memories. Enya, the Irish musician, even named one of her albums *The Memory of Trees*. So, the Celts might say, for example, that a particular tree is healing because someone was made well after sitting under it, and the tree retains the memory. Another might have psychiatric abilities, as it helped individuals overcome emotional or mental problems; and another tree is granted the memory of romantic love and relationships when a lover proposed to his betrothed under it, and so forth.

In granting the environment a living consciousness, the Celts straddle two worlds: the human one and the realm of the spirits of nature. In this way, they see the entirety of nature as a self-aware entity emitting a resonance that surrounds us.

My ol' teacher said that Merlin would walk in and out of this dimension through a tree, using it for his transition. At the time, he told me that I didn't have a clue what he meant by it. But 30 years later, I saw something very mysterious in the forest that I call the *Massive*. I've seen it four times. Imagine a spider that's 30 feet high and 60 feet across, moving in slow motion at one mile an hour. It has no body (it's invisible), but you can tell where it is, as it slightly bends reality when it passes by. It's staggering to watch! As it travels through the forest, it makes no effort to avoid trees and vegetation, walking right through trunks and branches as if they're not there.

While watching this, you soon realize that the environment isn't solid at all, and if you were standing inside the Massive, you'd be able to disappear into another dimension with ease. Perhaps every tree is a doorway, imbued with the memory of our history, standing as a silent record keeper of both the heroism of the human soul and its failings.

The idea of the memories of trees is interesting because, in effect, it resonates with the truth. We operate inside a sea of feelings emitted by nature, ourselves, and all the living beings surrounding us. To understand this concept is to incorporate your perceptions into a wider panorama. The trees become an ally, an imprint on your being. You take them with you when you leave the forest, just as the energy of animals follows you if you love them. It's a clear, fresh feeling which helps you, for you're not operating on a level playing field; we all exist within an unseen pulse of adverse energy. Perhaps you've always known that it was just about the hidden emotions of things but were scared to speak up. You feared being ridiculed or marginalized or that others would label you as dippy. However, you probably knew that you were right all along.

The world of commerce and constant striving—the one that we watch on TV—is composed of yang, ego, and intellect. It's usually the society of men whose achievements are lauded by other males and made special, which includes war, power, money, sexual conquest, fame, and so forth. These things are seen as important and praiseworthy, yet it's a warped mind-set, and the overall feeling is brown and ugly. This realm will be swept away—none of the yang will last. *Requiescat in pace, amen.* Only the softness of human feelings lasts, and perhaps that's what the Bible means in "the meek shall inherit the earth." Those sentiments are stored in your subconscious, which exists in two places—here and in the mirror-world.

The Perpetual Long-Term Memory of You

The mirror-self is, in effect, your soul. Like the memory of trees, it's the repository of your overall resonance. It's beautiful; and it's where the perpetual, long-term memory of you is kept. Here's how I came to an understanding of it: Ages ago I began to wonder what mechanism or recording device actually remembers you after the brain dies. Obviously, a lifetime of events and struggles here on Earth would be utterly meaningless if there were no way of recalling what happened. There couldn't be an afterlife without some sort of record, yet no religion or spiritual philosophy in the world that I know of has ever properly explained the technology of it. If there is life after death, what retains the perpetual remembering of you? Obviously, your brain can't hold that information once it ceases to function.

Via the Morph, I saw that we're all in the mirror-world before we die, in an alter ego functioning in an alternative dimension—your mirror-world identity. There are two of you: one who resides here and the other who is your subconscious counterpart, operating as your identity in the realm that we call the mirror-world. This solves the problem of what mechanism acts to retain the perpetual memory of you. Your mirror-self holds all of your life information, and it continues to exist as a separate identity in its own dimension with or without its other half, which is your waking mind and your physical body.

You're in the afterlife or the spirit world right now (if you want to call it that). That seems very technologically clever to me—problem solved. You don't have to carry your memories to an afterlife, as they're already there. In essence, your mirror-self is your soul, and in the Morph, you can actually see it moving through its world. Imagine how strange it is watching your soul-person operating independently from your waking mind; it doesn't seem credible at first, but there it is. The Bible talks of people losing their souls, and in a way, it's right. It can go missing in the sense that you rot your mirror-world self to a hellish state. Then again, if you paint it lovely, it will be beautiful.

As said, in the late 1920s, Paul Dirac discovered through mathematics a mirror-world of antiparticles that's opposite to this solid one. Later, his theories were tested and proven to be correct. Each particle (which is a unit of matter and energy) has an antiparticle, yet

Dirac's alternative realm doesn't look any different from our 3-D world except that there's an opposite charge. Your antiparticle self—sometimes known as the doppelganger—would look like your twin. The problem occurs if you shake hands with your double: You'd annihilate each other in a spectacular explosion.

It's thought that at the beginning of the Universe, the negatively charged antiparticles destroyed the positively charged ones, so what we see as our world are the remnants of those explosions. Because our universe is made up of only positive particles, scientists speculate that there must have been a slight excess of them over the negatively charged antiparticles. The ratio is estimated to be one extra positive in every billion particles. So, you're one in a million—well, a thousand million, actually.

The Mystical Kogi People

There's a precedent for the mirror-world idea. The mystical Kogi people of northern Colombia also believe in an alternative universe that they call the aluna. Special Kogi members are selected at birth to spend their first nine years in a cave, training to become visionaries. They live in the dark and aren't allowed to go into the outside world. This has the effect of altering their brain chemicals that fire DMT (dimethyltryptamine), a visionary element that's stored in the pineal gland in the brain. In this way, these magical children come to see the multidimensional mirror-world naturally. After nine years of training, the young people leave the cave to become the future mystics and spiritual leaders of the tribe, who are called *mamas*.

The Kogi trace their ancestors to the pre-Colombian Tairona people who were contemporaries of the Inca.

Like the Inca, the Kogi built stone stairs and platforms in the mountains that have resisted erosion for hundreds of years. They're a mystical people with a power that few others possess: the knowledge of a multidimensional world. They call the spirit of the aluna *puakari,* which the shamans pronounce *wha-car-ray.* They grant the mirror-world an identity, a consciousness much like the memory of trees.

To them, puakari is a great blessing. They say that whatever is seen in the spirit of the aluna happens here sooner or later, and a healing that occurs there becomes a physical healing in this world. They enter into the aluna performing medical procedures in that mirror-world, which affects the human body positively here.

They also use the aluna for protection. From there, they watched the Spanish conquistadors approaching. Aware of their location, the Kogi kept moving around the mountains of the Sierra Nevada de Santa Marta to avoid trouble. In this strange and wonderful way, they became the sole survivors of the conquistadors, who would have killed them for their gold. While all of the other indigenous tribes fell to the white man's diseases and violence, the Kogi thrived. They exist in a truly multidimensional Camelot that's hidden in our everyday world. Their ideas are pure and wonderful, and in the tribe's long history, they've never had a homicide. They don't usually permit outsiders to visit their mountain kingdom, although a British filmmaker was invited to produce a documentary about them in the 1990s.

The aluna is the place of the magical dimensions of Camelot that I've written about in the past. I'm happy now because I know how the dream will come about, for it's possible to not only become aware of the aluna but also to walk into it. I didn't realize that this could be done until one night I saw a man dematerialize just yards in front me. (I describe that incident later in the section where I talk about celestial beings in Chapter 5, so I'll leave it for the moment.) The fact is that the aluna knows you're coming years before you even get up out of your chair. Her spirit will call you if you have a warm heart and you're genuine about healing yourself and your shadow. But if you seek power and control, she'll act like the Kogi and hide. Sometimes she just tricks you, sending you in the wrong direction, but that's just her way of seeing how you'll respond.

The Mirror-World

The more I see the aluna, or the mirror-world, the more awesome it is to comprehend. Everything, including humans, came from there. We're conceived in the mirror-world, and that's where we'll return. I'm very content, for this is the first time in the 30 years of my journey that I can clearly see how we get to walk away to a happy place where peace is normal and where tomorrow's celebratory banquet was yesterday. For time in the aluna comes up from under your feet, and sometimes it twists to face you as a spiral might. When it does that, it goes the other way—backward. It's all very unusual but beautiful at the same time.

In the early '80s, when I figured out that there was a spirit world opposite to us, I wondered how to get there. So, I eventually built a mirrored room that was about seven feet high and wide. The mirrors were placed everywhere—the walls were covered as well as the floor and ceiling. I put my creation in a metal cage that I was going to hang from the ceiling, using a strong chain held by a mechanical car hoist. The idea was to have a floating, mirrored room to meditate in, and my goal was to peer into the spirit world (or worlds). However, I realized that I made a mistake in using metal to mount the mirrors. When temperature changes expanded and contracted the frame, it pulled the mirrors out of optical alignment. So, I wound up with a room of bendy mirrors like those you see at Disneyland and fun fairs. That was $5,000 down the gurgler in this dimension!

But once the Morph came, we found that we could view the mirror-world (aluna) without the help from any contraptions. What was mysterious was that we could see in there with our eyes open or shut. At first, we saw symbols: swirls and vortices and geometric shapes and patterns, moving up the walls of the sitting room. When we closed our eyes, we observed the same images traveling across our inner sight. So, the Morph symbols were simultaneously outside of us and within us.

From time to time, I'd see silver vortices of energy coming toward me from far off in the distance. They always traveled on a curved trajectory, which I found very interesting. If you look at the photo on the following page of a candle reflected in two mirrors, you can see that the refraction of light causes the candle to appear to be moving along a curved path.

Brigitte Wimmer

The curved trajectory of light reflected in two mirrors.

Of course, in this photo it appears this way because the stairway is curved, but if you place a candle between two mirrors, you'll see the trajectory that I speak of. It could be a coincidence, and then perhaps the curve is a factor of the refraction of the light's pathway from here to there.

Before the Morph came, I had quite a few experiences in what researchers called the near-death tube. I found that if you can entrance your mind into a virtual catatonic state, you can see up it without going through a clinical death. At that time I discovered that the near-death tube also has a distinct curve in it.

Because of the mirror-world, techniques like creative visualization, affirmations, and meditation—in which you process negative sentiments into positive feelings—are vital to your psychological and spiritual well-being. We affect how our mirror-person is energized by what we do over here. In other words, if you're down in the dumps for any length of time, the mirror-you suffers; and those emotions loop back onto you here, affecting you even further. Your negativity develops a transdimensional depth to it, and you find yourself in a spiral. In fact, I've come to see how the mirror-self, in essence, creates our life over here. Day to day, we act out our ideas as if our waking mind is in control, but mainly our actions are from subtle impulses coming from within. Certainly, we can countermand an impulse, but usually we don't.

In the Morph, the sight of the mirror-world became clearer, and although much of what I saw was in a rather dark setting, I could still make out what was happening. I'd see people moving in there, performing various, mundane functions. It's like peering into someone's home and watching him or her for a few seconds. At times, I'd troll through what seemed like a hundred suburban houses one after the next—all in the mirror-world. I'd look and move on, sometimes seeing individuals cooking dinner or whatever; then often, the places seemed vacant. It's weird to me that there are such ordinary things in the spirit world (like neighborhoods), but it's a mirror image of this one, so that's probably why it appears the way it does.

Eventually, I started to see myself in that mirror-world. It was a bit frightening there in the early days, as it seemed that I was always under attack and seriously outnumbered. However, I brought it upon myself in this lifetime by sticking my neck out and challenging the norm. I always had a lot of problems with the standard beliefs, and I wanted to discover more and prove it all for myself. If you go against the system, there are unseen energies here and in the mirror-world that will fight you to protect their status quo and the control that they have over humans and their evolution. That's why the world of the fringe dweller is always a bit fraught—especially if you talk about it to others—for the fact that you're walking away to another reality threatens them. It somehow casts doubts on what they believe, which can make them antagonistic . . . keep it to yourself is my advice.

To cut a long story short, in the first days of watching the mirror-world, it was as if I were continually being set upon by a gang of hoodlums with no proper way to defend myself. I was a victim of my inadequacy. The motion of my person in that world was very slow; it was like moving through wet sand. Every action took forever, while my attackers seemed to be going at normal speed, so I had no defense whatsoever. That nasty situation lasted six months, and I hated every moment of it. It caused me a lot of psychological distress, as what was happening there blipped into my life and feelings over here. I had a lot of unexplainable pain in my body that seemed to appear mysteriously from nowhere. I believe that it came from being attacked over there in the mirror-world.

Many of the women I knew at the time would tell me about strange bruises on their legs that appeared overnight. Sometimes they were circular and about the size of a nickel, and others were a bit bigger, closer to the size of a quarter. On different occasions, the ladies got red triangular marks that stung slightly. No one could explain it, except that there's a perpetual fight going on between humans headed for the light and the malevolent beings who are trying to intimidate or hold us back. But no amount of evil can come at you if you don't harbor a part of that darkness inside yourself, so that's why we need to clean up and move to better ground. It's part of the heroic property of our souls: the desire to reach for a celestial place. We may not be qualified to arrive there just yet, but we must seek it no matter how imperfect we are. There's absolution for everyone in this life—even the worst.

To conclude this segment, I can say that I'm almost positive that you'll see the Morph sooner or later because it's everywhere. There's a mechanism of alignment that's available to you, and it's in the knowing—in the "click" of your mind. (The worst way is that you'll have to visit me at one of my seminars, and I'll show you.) With these items in your possession, you'll be able to access that doorway. Eventually you should be able to cross to those other worlds just by knowing about them. It will come to you, as it's a tilt of the mind whereby you suddenly see what others don't. It doesn't take a rocket scientist, but it does require a certain amount of courage. I've said before that there are places deep inside yourself that you have to discover and unearth; you must allow them to come out in order to comprehend them. But that's all part of the heroic compassion of self that I spoke of and an understanding that none of us is perfect. We're all white and some black. So, as a spirit, you're mostly gray, neither a saint nor a devil—someplace in between.

We're all fallen angels doing our best to transcend and redeem ourselves. We don't seek perfection; there's no such thing. We only pursue this, and hopefully we'll help others realize the same peace and reconciliation, for that's the precious gift we have to offer those in our life: deliverance. It's what I call the Third Principle. There's light and also darkness; and the third principle is deliverance, whereby you walk away from the turmoil to an eternal now—free from pain. This is a present waiting for you that will take you beyond the reach of the dark forces (human or transdimensional) who want to feed off you and send you the wrong way. It's a liberation from despair, confusion, and misunderstanding, back to the light and an eternal happiness and peace.

As I see it, deliverance is the act of reversing your perspectives and walking the other way, and redemption is the process of reconciling the light and the dark within—becoming whole again. To that end, you need personal information, which can't be found in books because they're more general. So, you look to the meditative state for answers, and you lie still and wait to see what visions and advice is offered. There's a mechanism at work here, an inner power to assist you.

I'd like to talk some more about the memory of things, and the resonance that you leave behind as you move along. Let's go to a new chapter.

RESONANCE AND THE SOUND OF YOUR SOUL

The soul, the mirror-you, holds the perpetual memory of you. It emits a resonance, which is an imprint in a force field, a wave pattern—imagine it as a sound wave. That unique tone is ancient and mysterious, and I believe that the essence of each of us existed before the Universe began. Certainly, the vibration is at a level that surpasses anything we've ever heard here on Earth. And beyond the mirror-world are other realms: Each of us is spread throughout the layers of eternity like stripes of chocolate though the center of a sponge cake.

The source of that celestial resonance on Earth is your heart. It throbs out the feelings that are remembered in your soul, and those are initially emitted from your heart chakra. It's a pulse or a signal—one that's "you" shaped. It moves fast, traveling through the etheric wave that surrounds your body and then out to others. Those signals that you give off imprint reality around you, just as Professor Emoto's water crystals are changed into beautiful snowflake shapes or horrible, disfigured images, depending on the feeling of the word that's written on the glass tube containing the water.

If your heart is big, you're open, generous, and loving; and you've come to accept humanity unconditionally and without judgment, proving it by serving others, then the tone of your soul could resonate for many miles right across a city. You'd have the silent power to bend what's become unbalanced and dark back to beauty and symmetry. When the heart tone is beautiful, its resonance is very deep. The closest sound here in our world is that of a Tibetan bowl. I don't think that they actually come from Tibet anymore (the hippies make them), but they're lovely and easy to find in New Age shops or on the Internet. You can hear how their resonance, especially the crystal ones', carries you off to another place. It's a healing tone. If you listen carefully, you can feel yourself going down the center of the calming sound and into another dimension.

Let's look at your etheric energy and discover what can be done to make it prettier and more resonant. By raising the vibration to oscillate faster, we hope to disengage from disease and discord and align to a more pure and beautiful life. Let's try to listen to the song of your soul—its stately otherworld imprint, if you like—and see if we can intuit what it's like. But first, I want to talk about your etheric fields and the biophotons that make it up.

Your Etheric Web as Packets of Light

Twenty years ago, I discovered that I could view the etheric field around trees, and I've written about it in my other books. You'll see that it's no big deal—it just involves practice, and you need to develop your peripheral vision, as etheric light is very faint, and only the rods at the side of your eyes can observe it. When looking straight ahead, mentally take your concentration to what's beside you without moving your eyes. Doing so will gradually activate the rods over time.

After I saw the etheric around trees, I eventually noticed it around humans and animals. And finally when my ability to view it grew stronger, I realized that it's around everything—plants, bugs, and so on. The etheric is full of fast-moving vortices and striations of hazy light. Later, I came to see several complicated ramifications in the fields. In many ways, author Carlos Castaneda was right when he said that we walk around in a luminous egg, as the etheric stretches out from each of us for several feet in all directions. Its weakest area is below the knees, but it's strong around the upper body and extends a foot or so above the head because of the closeness to the brain and heart, of course.

Our sentiments make impressions on the field and bend it. As I said in my book *Sixth Sense* (which was published by Hay House), what we normally describe as feelings are just sensations—electrical pulses in the brain. So, if you tap the back of your hand with your knuckle, a signal is sent to your brain warning you of potential pain. Our perception of life is encoded in a series of electrical pulses; and what we call emotions are our reactions to those pulses, such as pleasure, pain, happiness, and anger. But real human feelings of love, hate, frustration, joy, and so forth reside in the etheric. This is why you can read people accurately and sometimes help them. You pick up on the hidden feelings they emit by touching their etheric with your mind or placing your hand on their chest. I know that many of you understand exactly what I'm talking about.

Meanwhile, here's a bit of the scientific background to the etheric field. Researchers discovered a new particle, a very weak one called a biophoton that's measured using very sensitive equipment. Biophotons are part of the light spectrum that appears to be given off by all living things. It's thought to be light emitted from the DNA. The discovery of biophotons seems to confirm the existence of the etheric field around our bodies as scientific fact.

A photon is a quantum of light. So, a biophoton is a particle of light given off by a biological (living) system, such as the human body. The light emanating from a glowworm is another example. Medical scientists in Russia discovered the biophoton in 1923 and originally gave it the strange name of "mitogenetic rays." But nothing much came of it until it was rediscovered by the German biophysicist Fritz-Albert Popp, who theorized that the glow originates from DNA and has a coherent quality—meaning that it's organized, like laser light.

The *chi* flowing in our body's energy channels (known as meridians), which is used in Chinese medicine, may well be related to power lines or force fields in an organism's biophoton field. The *prana* of Hindu mystics may also be a way of using our breath to direct the electromagnetic biofields researched by Professor Popp. In other words, the basis of acupuncture is the flow of lines in the etheric, which, of course, is a field of cohesive information. The reason why laser light travels a long distance is because the particles are tightly bound together, so the light doesn't spread out and dissipate like the beam of a flashlight. That type of unity is the same for the etheric light around your body. That's why you can fire your etheric using your concentration and the power of your will. You can send it across the street, and someone who can see it even a little bit can watch you do it.

Professor Popp suggested that certain diseases may be due to a drop-off in resonance of the biophotons emitted by the body. I'm almost sure that he's right because when people begin to get sick, I've noticed that the etheric field around their faces starts to go hazy, as if a faint fog surrounds them. Now even if you can't see the etheric, you can still tell where a physical difficulty exists. If your mind is calm, you'll be drawn to where the etheric is slower in another body. Just a couple of nights ago, I looked at a friend of mine and my attention went to his belly. I wondered what was wrong, and without my saying anything, he later told me that he was experiencing low-grade pain in his colon. (When the colon aches, it's often because it's swollen, restricting flow. The trick is to avoid bread, alcohol, and an excess of meat, which is very acidic. Colonic irrigation usually fixes it.)

It's been suggested that people are influenced by remote sources of etheric light, which has led to research into distant healing. This explains why certain magical healers can either breathe on or touch people and cure them. That's also why we seek to raise the energy of the etheric and make it go faster. In theory, the biophotons of the etheric field can't be seen by the naked eye, but in subdued light, it's clearly visible. As I mentioned, there are thousands of people all over the world who view it regularly.

I've never thought that the sight of it took any particular spiritual or psychic gift. As I've written in my books, all you have to do is tilt your head slightly when viewing things in minimal light—say, looking at a tree at dusk. Focus on the top of a tree, and then move your attention a little way to the right and stare at the sky there. Without shifting your eyes, take your concentration back to the top of the tree, and you'll see the tree's "life-field," as now its light is coming to your eyes at a slight angle. It's not hard to pick up. Find a big leafy tree such as an oak that has a lot of energy—not a wispy thing like an aspen. The more branches and leaves it has, the greater the field that will burst into your view all around.

Use the same angled-view technique when looking for the etheric around humans: Tilt your head slightly and you'll see it. This is necessary because the cones at the center of your eyes can't see as well as the rods on the sides. It's easy to remember: C for cones and center, and R for . . . oh, well, never mind.

Peripheral vision engages the rods, which are more acute than our normal "straight-on" vision. So, etheric sight is nothing more than the habit of strengthening the rods in your eyes and tilting your head slightly to allow a diffused light source to enter your eye at an angle. You can't see the etheric well in bright or neon lights. You need to look for it at dusk or under a soft lighting. It's very much like the Morph in this way. In fact, the etheric looks exactly like it except the Morph is even more powerful and lively. It's possible that the Morph that descended in March 2001 is nothing more than Earth's etheric, descending lower and closer, in order to save the planet before humanity overwhelms and destroys it. Some say that Gaia is the feminine spirit of nature—the very soul of our world—and she's the controlling energy that forms part of the earth's self-knowing. And it knows what's needed to defend itself from pollution and degradation.

If you're interested in morphogenesis and the fields of information around living things, such as the etheric, you might want to check out the work of British biologist Rupert Sheldrake. (Some of his articles are posted on my Website, **www.stuartwilde.com**, in the section marked *Learn*.) Sheldrake says that we're all surrounded by fields of information that he calls morphogenetic fields, which direct the way an organism develops. So, a giraffe is "giraffe shaped" because it's enclosed by an entity containing the history of all the giraffes that have ever lived on Earth. And a baby one grows from inside that field of information, and it learns "giraffe things" from that inherent memory. In a way, it's back to the memory of trees. (I interviewed Sheldrake once. He's very genuine—I liked him.)

Professor Popp also speculated that biophotons are message carriers and may be responsible for ESP and nonlocal jumps of information in quantum fields. I'm absolutely sure that's right. I don't want to get too complicated here, but I experienced very dramatic proof of our ability to affect physical reality at a distance. Let me tell you the tale because it's an easier way to understand how you imprint life than delving deeply into Professor Popp's theories, which I must say are very valid, yet they're not necessarily written for the layperson.

Etheric Imprints on the Skin

Shortly after the Morph showed up in 2001, I was in a castle in Tuscany, Italy, with a group of seminar participants when my skin began to prickle. (You may wind up having the same Morph sensation yourself. It's quite common and doesn't hurt, but it does take a while to get used to it, as it makes you itch quite a bit.) As the prickling started, I noticed that pictures were forming on my hands and arms: triangles and circles; Christian crosses and holy words, such as prayers in Latin; and images of small animals, children's faces, pretty flowers, and so forth.

It would take about 20 minutes for a picture to fully morph into view on my hands or arms. They often looked like they were drawn with a brown crayon, but then sometimes the lines that delineated them were pure white. The pigment of my suntanned skin was somehow changed in a matter of minutes into clear lines, as if a drawing was bleached into my skin as an imprint. The whole process was very mystical, and some of the pictures were truly mind-boggling. Most were quite small—a square inch, say—and some were almost 18 inches across, like the one that appeared on my chest and reminded me of a crop circle that I'd seen in Wiltshire, England, a few years before. The image that morphed onto me was a geometric spiral, coming from the Julia set (a type of fractal in mathematics). There were also other fractal patterns that appeared, such as the Fibonacci spirals and the famous lying-down Buddha of the Mandelbrot set.

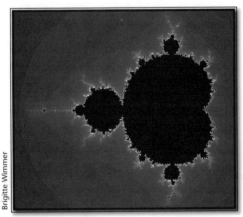

Brigitte Wimmer

The lying-down Buddha of the Mandelbrot set.

You watch an image like this appear on your chest from nowhere, and then you wonder if the next picture you'll see is of the men in white coats who have those canvas jackets that lace up at the back! A friend of mine has a venture called The Academy of Everything Is Possible, and I think I must have joined without knowing it. Anyway, as peculiar as this story may be, 50 or more people witnessed the images. They weren't undefined—they were very clear. They lasted anywhere from 20 minutes to several hours before they faded, although a few of the white ones are still faintly visible five years later. Sometimes my skin would immediately start to prickle again, and the first image would morph and change from one picture to another. The sweetest image I can remember was a lion cub with a halo. The phenomenon of these visions on my skin lasted nonstop for five months, coming and going 24/7 and appearing all over but mainly on my hands, arms, chest, and back. There were more than 10,000 of them during that time. And then they slowed down and within a few days, stopped completely.

The whole process was utterly mysterious. I never understood it, and I haven't really experienced it again in large quantities like that, although one or two appear from time to time—not often. But I've seen the pictures forming on other people since mine ceased in November 2001. What was really interesting was that the images were imprints in the etheric, as if I was a canvas being painted on. I've come to wonder if crop circles are the same thing—an etheric cookie cutter, stamping itself onto the landscape.

The idea of using your mind to imprint reality was confirmed to us because we found that for a few days at least, anyone could draw on my skin just by using thoughts. I'd sit on my bed with my shirt off, and my friends would stand around and think of a pattern.

They'd tell me what it was and where on my upper chest and arms they wanted to put it—say, two triangles with a circle laced in between each other on the upper left arm. Then they'd project it mentally toward me from about two or three yards away. I'd feel the prickling sensation start up, and the images would form in a matter of minutes. It was heaps of fun. My friends discovered that they could do it over and over again without fail, but the power of that mental projection only lasted a brief time before it went away. It was strange! It came to show us the impressions that humans make, and we acknowledged it. People imprint us, and we do the same to them.

There was something even more intriguing during that time of the patterns on my skin: If a small flower such as a primrose started to appear on the back of my hand, we'd also all see it in the Morph as a shadow gradually drifting up the wall of the room we were in. So, that's how I came to realize that the pictures were inside of me coming out onto my skin, and they were also on the outside as visible images in the room.

In other worlds, you're a transmitting and receiving station of etheric downloads and imprints. Some are graphic, others are mental, and many are in the buzz or formatting sound that I spoke of earlier. There's much information that you may not be aware of, and that's a part of the wonderful story going on in your soul, unfolding from deep within. You should never worry about where you'll go and how you'll get there in this life—you'll always know . . . trust.

And the more you align to a soft world and spiritual way, the more you'll see it all come miraculously into your life. Four other people I know of experienced the pictures on their skin—sometimes more than once. So, the idea of an etheric imprint on our humanity is much like Emoto's water crystals. It's certainly true from my perspective. Then you can see how the Morph and the supernatural is outside of us and inside as well. *We're all in the Morph, and it's in us.* The record of your life so far is in there, and your future possibilities are also there in all their glory, even though it may be somewhat hazy to you right now. We're all in a hologram—possibly, the whole universe is one—and you're in my molecule, and I'm in yours. That might be a critical realization for all of us one day.

The Karma Loop

You're in a karma loop, which is shaped like a Pringles potato chip. I'm not mad on Pringles—they smell funny. Anyway, what goes around comes around in the great Pringles tube in the sky. . . .

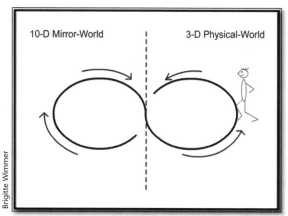

The saddle-shaped karma loop.

We all have a rudimentary understanding of that loop effect as we experience it day to day, but what's the technical reason for energy and karma coming back to us? Your mind imprints your etheric biophotons, and they go out as light, imprinting reality around you—especially other people, who are mainly made of water. Those individuals will react negatively or positively, and as you respond to their reactions, you release subtle feelings into your mirror-self, adding to your stored memories. And through them, your mirror-self changes. It tends to drift back and forth in the mirror-world landscape to those parts (geographies) that reflect its/your current state. So, it will go from a hellish realm to a blissful one, and then back to the nightmarish world.

Gradually the mirror-self starts to pump energy back toward you here in the physical world, and that reflects in your body and mind. In effect, it's the return envelope of what you put out emotionally and mentally into your etheric weeks ago. Eventually you're required to take your own stuff back as an energy manifestation in your physical body. Pain, disease, and perhaps a lack of luminosity are the consequences of the karma loop. Perhaps all disease starts in the mind, traveling through our etheric and into the mirror-world, where the impulse intensifies and then bounces back. In other words, is today's headache a result of last week's feelings? A lot of it comes initially from being afraid. It's weird that our evolution has so much to do with processing fear.

Etheric Moves for Processing and Transcending Fear

First, you should never be ashamed of your fears. We humans are small and fragile, poised as we are in an enormous universe. Any one of a dozen things can take us out in an instant. Yet overcoming fear is part of learning to love, for we can't love properly when we're afraid. Fear leaves no space for such positive emotions; it swamps your mind and closes your heart, and your etheric goes gray and dull looking. The wider you become, the more vulnerable you are—it's a test. By letting go and opening up, you allow yourself to be in greater danger and uncertainty and are more likely to be ripped off, and of course, ridiculed. Yet can you live forever in the tight environment of the ego's fears and the rules that it imposes upon you? Can you truly express yourself as a complete person, a lovely and spiritual person, if you don't take risks, trust in others, and go for it? The only way forward is bit by bit, as fast as you can accommodate any insecurity.

Here's something that I've mentioned before elsewhere. An English shaman taught it to me, and it's worth retelling for those who don't know it. Most persistent low-grade fear isn't a result of psychological issues or a poor state of well-being. It's often due to dehydration. Most people don't drink nearly enough water, and the water in alcohol and other beverages doesn't count. We need about six pints a day, which is just less than three liters. Otherwise, body cells become dehydrated, and apprehension and insecurity dramatically increase. I don't know why this causes fear and anxiety, but it's been observed to do so. Most people wouldn't be scared or depressed if they were better hydrated.

If you consume enough water, you'll see a dramatic improvement in a short time. In addition to six pints, you should also take three lecithin tablets, or three tablespoons of the granules, spread out during the day. (You'll find lecithin at health-food shops.) The lecithin helps cells absorb water. Once you start, you'll notice a

substantial reduction in your levels of anxiety after about three days. In total, it takes about three weeks to properly rehydrate the body. After that, remember to maintain your water intake, and increase it whenever you feel the uneasiness creeping back. The hydration discipline is simple to do, gets rid of low-grade fear, and helps with mild cases of depression.

Discipline Your Mind

As you rein in the ego and begin to control it, your life becomes less fearful. Meditation helps a lot, for it's the only way to properly discipline the mind and stop it from thinking so much. Many people suffer from mental diarrhea—overthinking makes you queasy. The less you worry, the more open you become, allowing etheric light to infuse within you. And the less energy you waste and burn, the more transcendent and self-confident you'll feel.

Sometimes fear comes from suffering a drop in vitality, which may be etheric—mental or physical. Either way, a lack of discipline and too much low-energy stuff (confrontation, for example) set up the fear of collapse. That's why the unknown poses a problem for some people. They worry that they may not be able to sustain themselves—financially, physically, or emotionally—in different circumstances. However, when you're powerful, you can express that might wherever you go. Changing locations and circumstances means little to you, for you're strong within yourself.

If you're insecure, here's a fast review of tried and tested things that you can immediately begin doing:

1. Exercise every day for 20 minutes, if you can. Even gentle movement like walking is better than nothing at all. If you don't exercise, you'll get scared.

Remember that extra fat in your body is stored fear or pain: ancient memories that are held in your flesh. Certainly, we all put on a bit of weight in middle age, but you must lose it by the time you get to your late 50s or early 60s, as there aren't very many old fat people. To be healthy, you have to be a normal weight.

I'd be the last person to offer you a weight-loss diet. I'm sure that you're fed up with all the fads and hype surrounding them, except to say that almost all the transcendental people whom I know—the true Morph warriors—are vegetarians. They don't like to kill to survive or ingest the fear that's in the meat of the animal's body, so most of them live substantially on organic, raw foods. In this state, the food is alive—it has light in it. I'm not an expert on these things, and I've cooked food in the winter when it's cold, but I go to a diet that has lots of raw food as the spring comes along. If you want to study up on this, check out the books by David Wolfe. Enough said on that topic.

2. Try to rest and sleep. So many achievers and high-action, modern parents suffer from sleep deprivation. Insomnia causes low-grade fear. Repose whenever you can; and when you do, make sure you're in a darkened room, as the immune system operates less efficiently if you're always surrounded by light. Also, allow yourself at least an hour a day of quiet time to ponder your life and your strongest moves. It's a time to dream while awake, and not doing this can make you anxious—it's just like

a lack of sleep. Life requires us to be brave. Nurturing yourself, resting, and being calm and in control develops security and personal strength.

Having less responsibility and fewer activities also helps. See what you can get rid of. If your life is too cluttered, you soon lose yourself and become scattered. I know so many people who sold up and quit the life of the yuppie whirl—they took their little suitcase and floated off to discover themselves. Of course, if you have a family and children, you may not be able to do that right now, but maybe you can adjust your life to be less active. We often work hard to pay the bills, and that act creates more expenses. We buy things, but if you think about it, everything you own in the end winds up owning you. Sorry, I can't remember who first said that, but he or she is right.

I learned a lot about the nature of terror and fear as a fire-walking instructor. My associates and I walked about 8,000 individuals over the years, and it was interesting to observe how people handle the unknown. Right before they started, I'd tell them that their ego would quit and seemingly leave, and they'd function as if in a dream, often not recalling what happened. I'd explain that this sensation was a result of the sull (a hypnotic trance), which is induced by fear. And because of this state of mind, they'd probably want to walk the fire twice. Few believed me! Yet on every occasion, about 65 percent of the participants would do it a second time.

Life is often like the moment just before a fire walk: Fear wipes your consciousness of the experience of living, and you enter a self-induced trance. Life passes you by, as years slip away without you ever discovering your true self. Time flies when you're stuck in the mud.

Awareness is a gift granted to the courageous. You can't get rid of fear entirely, but you can come into control of your mind. And by disciplining yourself, you'll feel more confident and secure—it's not hard. Being afraid is a bad habit, but it's one that each of us can learn to handle. Here's a quickie: If you suffer from nightmares, stop eating protein after about six in the evening, as most bad dreams are a result of consuming rich foods. So, eat very light at night—no heavy stuff, steaks, and so on.

Nifty Etheric Moves

Here are some worthwhile etheric tricks that I've mentioned in other writings. They're nifty when you feel yourself becoming scared.

1. Make a fist and thump yourself fairly forcefully in the sternum (center of the chest) as many times as it takes to change the energy of the heart chakra. This will open it to more energy. But don't punch too hard! The sternum is quite fragile, so be sure to hit just hard enough to effect change.

2. Put your thumb and your first two fingers together on both hands, and tap your cheeks simultaneously, an inch or so below your eyes. Do this vigorously and quickly. There's a meridian there, and this action changes the energy flow. You'll feel it!

3. Put one hand over the other, and place them upon your navel, gently pressing inward. You can do this lying down on your back if you wish. Etherically, fear flows out of the solar plexus, gushing like rain through a storm

pipe. But putting your hands over your navel stems the loss of energy, and the less energy you lose, the calmer you'll be.

4. Lock the fingers of your hands together, and place them on the top of your head across the middle (covering your crown chakra). Pull your arms downward, pressing yourself toward the ground. This motion guides your etheric back and inhibits your imagination from flying off the handle, taking your crown chakra upward. If this chakra tries to go too high, hysteria and symptoms of madness set in.

If a child is agitated, just place your hand firmly on the top of the little one's head and press down. Lightly hold your other hand against the child's navel and press inward—both hands working together simultaneously. The hand on the head is good for calming and getting kids off to sleep. You can also etherically touch children from a distance, as long as you can see them. Imagine yourself with an extended arm: Mentally see yourself reaching out, placing your hand on the child's head and pressing down firmly, using the authority of your will.

5. If you're very panicky—say, you've done too many drugs or you're overly speedy and out of control with anxiety—lie on the ground with your head to the north and feet to the south (in the dirt is best). Try to get as much of your skin in contact with the ground as possible. If conditions permit, take all or most of your clothes off. Visualize pushing the fear down through your body into the ground, anchoring it. Say, "Mother Earth, I'm giving you back this fear of mine." An alternative is to allow natural running water to flow down your spine—lying

down in a stream, for example. The water trick also works when you feel your energy dropping, such as when you're getting the flu or whatever. Take a nice warm shower, and once you're hot, quickly flip it to just the cold water. Let that run down your spine, and then go back to hot and then back to cold. Do it four to six times if you can stand it—at least three times, anyway. This process kicks the immune system into action, waking it up.

I can't tell you how many times I'd be on a lecture tour and feel wasted and sick. I'd use the cold shower as an emergency measure an hour or two before I was scheduled to be up onstage. It really works! (Here's a sidebar: If you have a pet—especially a dog—you shouldn't hold or touch it if you're feeling scared or emotionally upset, as your furry friend may suck the emotion through the etheric and become sick.)

6. A quick way to reduce fear is to imagine it as a lump of dough on your chest. Just grab it with your hand and toss it to one side. This works.

In conclusion, all fear at its psychological base is the abhorrence of loss or death—not necessarily physical death, but the death of things that we're comfortable with: our relationships, a job, perhaps a familiar situation that's about to shift, or whatever. If you haven't already done so, train your mind to see change as beneficial and necessary. Nothing persists forever, so don't hold on. Prepare to release, and allow the law of flow to come into your life.

On Being of Service

Do you see where we're going with all of this? It's an uncoupling process. First, we looked at your inner self and the existence of the additional mirror-world self. And then you saw the clusters that you're in and how they hold you. You glimpsed the possible liberation of your soul, and to that end, we gazed at the imprint of "you" on reality as you go along.

What's your purpose here? That could be answered by, "I work and pay rent, buy food, shovel it in, and pass it out; and then I toil some more, rushing about accumulating things until I have no more energy—then I'll die." But if that's so, what kind of purpose is there in it? Most people are just taking up space and generating pollution. It makes you wonder how long the soul, or Gaia, of the planet is going to stand for that! You can see how in developing a higher purpose, you build a spiritual identity beyond the mundane. You begin to return the energy you consume from Gaia—it's debt repayment. It seems to me that the purpose of your life should be this: First, use your income to buy opportunities for yourself so that you have knowledge and experiences that you can share with others. Then surely the main purpose of your life is to be of service. I don't mean just helping children and family members, but also serving humanity and animals—service to this planet.

All that will count for anything when you die won't be how many mortgage checks you paid or how much money you left to your family, but what you did for this planet. Whom did you serve? How much did you love and help those you touched? Through service we operate from our heart space and install light energy into the hologram of life. It's a bridge that we build for people and ourselves. It might seem as if you're supporting others, but in fact, you're learning to honor and care for the eternity within you. It's a form of remembering, like the memories of trees—a higher remembering that's imprinted in your soul.

We all belonged to a special event—a higher knowing that we forgot about, and I can't say when it occurred. Maybe it was 15,000 years ago, or perhaps there's no sense of time in that far dimension, so we can't say if it was 15,000 or even a million years ago. But we have the memory of the knowing, as it's inside of us. An Italian friend of mine calls it "a nostalgia for eternity." It's in the beauty of that nostalgia that we faintly remember where we came from. It's like a signpost taking us back to what we already know in our ancient memory. Remember, the essence of every human on Earth is older than the Universe.

We're raised to think that life is all about us and how cozy and comfortable we can become, but if you believe that, then you've been a bit misled or at best, you haven't gotten to a sophisticated grip of things. It may not be your fault. You might well be lost in concepts that you've been spoon-fed to trap you. In fact, I'd like to suggest that this life has little to do with you, except in the marginal sense that you must care for your day-to-day upkeep. But your real journey starts elsewhere. Focusing on you and your needs is okay, but it's not the be-all and end-all of your life's purpose. You may have had an inkling of this over the years. Spirit may have talked to you in quiet moments, while the part of your mind that thinks it's running the show was laboring under its grand delusion.

Yes, the mind pretends to rule your life, but that's all part of the con. It controls very little even though it will insist the opposite. What is the mind? It's just a data bank of ideas and concepts—a cat's cradle of erroneous facts for the most part. The intellect is useful, but it also holds you back. You can become part of something much bigger and more glorious once you're able give yourself away. I'm sure you'll see it. I've often said that the spiritual journey through life is just four feet long. You travel one foot down from your head to your heart and three feet outward to embrace the first human you meet. That's the ivory tower coming down, which then allows you a tactile contact with the reality of humanity and its very soul.

In the end, it's all about deliverance, and that's more important than anything else in the world. You save yourself from forgetfulness. Then, you deliver others who are drawn to you, for if you don't, who will? Many don't have much of a chance without you. Think of that . . . nil! There are those whom you know or will meet later in life who can't escape unless you agree to help. You're their only chance, and they'll never meet anyone else who knows the secret. They can't escape because most people can't see beyond the mind. It's a terrible thing that they have no ancient recall.

Now you might say, "Listen up, Stuie bubba! This deliverance business is a bit dodgy. Why do I need it?" And I'd reply that most people care little for it, but that's mainly because they can't see what's in their subconscious, and they have no clue as to what's waiting up the road, so to speak. We're surrounded by the world of the ghouls, and they're between the molecules of this reality looking to entice and trap people. It's a war of control—that is, dominion over the human mind. Trust me . . . you need deliverance! And of course, the more people start remembering, the more the ghouls will lose their domination. So, if you give it a go, it helps us all.

I know some think that if they join one religion or another, they'll be instantly saved, but that idea is fraught with problems. A religion can offer hope, and it may promise an elitist deliverance, but no such thing exists. It's a bit of a ghoul trap. No one can give you eternity unless you hold the nostalgia of it. It has to be in your mind night and day—a yearning in your soul. I've heard it described as an ache to return home. Religion isn't necessarily the answer, for your imprint is a feeling, not the outcropping of a dogma.

I know a mafioso type. Deep down he's okay, but he's been abusive and violent all his life, fighting and causing others pain. Inflicting damage gave him a thrill. He's sexist and a virulent racist, making no bones about shouting out his harsh ideas in the company of others. He's a devoted Roman Catholic, and he's also scared of death. But he believes that his religion will save him, and he'll go to heaven because he's supported the church, attended Mass, and tagged along, so to speak. I fear he may be in for a rude awakening. . . .

I try to love him, and he does have redeeming qualities in that he's very funny and generous to some people—those he's not trying to hurt, anyway. But that, like his religion, is his outer mask. His inner self is like something out of *The Sopranos* TV show, and he's staying in that cluster until he dies. He's as ghoul infested and transdimensionally abducted as it gets. He sees himself as holy and good, yet his imprint on life is ugly and dark. His mirror-self is trapped. It's as if he's possessed of an evil without ever knowing it. It hides in his soul, and he

lives in the section of the mirror-world reserved for those who express power by hurting others, using fear to reign supreme. They think they're special. Religion, influence, and money drive that illusion.

We live in a sea of energy. You're a snowflake, a beautiful crystalline structure. Or, are you a demonic pulse of evil polluting everything and making people sick as you walk past them in the street? Religion doesn't count for much if the feeling isn't there. But if you put out a truly soft imprint and you love the world, then everything you touch or breathe upon has the basis of the remembering because you learned. The next person who grasps the same shopping cart that you used may also begin to recall. It's the heart space or tone that you leave behind, and everywhere you go becomes a doorway for others. They'll sit on the same bench that you sat on, and their mind will drift. And they'll slide to 90 degrees without knowing it, suddenly hearing the faint sound of their soul calling, asking them to step away from the cold, tightness, and pain, to a new freedom. Then they start to remember.

On Silent Talking

Thoughts jump. How many times have you been pondering something obscure, and then the person next to you mentions the very thing that's been on your mind? Silent communication generally comes about when you're thinking in the direction of another person, rather than concentrating inwardly toward your own thoughts and emotions. You have to set your mind to one side and concentrate on others.

Silent communication to the human soul can be in the form of prayers or nonverbal affirmations for the well-being of others. Then there's actual mental dialogue that's spoken silently in the direction of another individual. It's a telepathic transfer of energy, and hopefully it's a sweet message that offers love or encouragement of some sort. In Paris recently, I was watching a middle-aged lady walking into a café; she looked a bit stressed-out. In my mind, I asked her, *Are you afraid?* She turned toward me and nodded. I kept going and asked, *Are you sick?* She shook her head. So, I breathed love into her heart. She passed behind me and took a seat. Minutes later, a tall man in his 70s came by, and he looked like he was in pain. I inquired silently, *Do your lungs hurt?* He grabbed his shirt with his right hand and looked at me helplessly. It was the look of a small child begging a grown-up for assistance. My inner response to him was to drink lots of water, as I felt that it would help him.

One day I was walking through the customs hall at the Philadelphia airport and an official stopped me, wanting to search my metal flight case that I was carrying. Mentally, I touched him on the side of the head and projected a soft, warm feeling that said, "It's safe. I need to go now, thank you." He hesitated, but then pointed to the case, as if requesting that I open it. Again, I silently replied that it's safe and I needed to go now. He pulled his hand back and asked, "Are those computers?"

I answered audibly, "Yes, sir."

"Okay," he said and waved me through. Of course, he wouldn't have let me go if I had a nefarious darkness in my feelings—he would have felt it.

When you talk silently to people, look at their right temple and blank your mind. Then just tap them with your thought—like reaching out with your hand to touch them on the side of the head. Expel a short, sharp breath as the thought goes across, the more quiet and nonchalant the better. The harder you try, the less effective you are. Soft and subtle, that's the way. Morphic resonance is the language of force fields interacting with each other. Your brain is a complex one that stores and receives information in the form of wave packets. We have a holographic brain inside a holographic universe; there's no distance between anything. When you talk silently to another, you are, in effect, talking to yourself.

Once you can achieve this, observe people's reactions. See if they twitch slightly or make facial movements, as those tell you that there are pulses coming through to them from the mirror-worlds. If you've ever watched newsreels of Hitler's speeches, you might have noticed the strange twitches that he made as he spoke—surges of evil from deep within. Sometimes people don't do it, though, and instead, they move their eyes upward and to the right, which usually means that they're entering a mild trance at about seven cycles a second. If the incoming pulse is pain related, they might wince ever so surreptitiously. You'll learn that as you ask a question, they'll show you their reply, just like the man with the lung trouble was grabbing his shirt.

Look at eyes and lips carefully. Often, that's where you can read a person's history. Try for the obvious first, for persistent emotions over many years etch the shape of a person's lips. Anger is easy to spot, as is arrogance. Pompous people raise their heads back ever so slightly, as if the nasty smell of lesser beings is under their nose. The tilt is a subconscious attempt to establish height over others. Violent individuals have a madness in the eyes and give off a strange asymmetrical bend in their etheric that looks like a curved line at the outer edge of the field, like this: (. It comes from the threat they offer, as it's part of the desire to lean over and manipulate people. The need to control is a form of insanity. It's the first symptom of demonic possession, which often deteriorates into physical and emotional abuse.

When a person is becoming spiritually insane—meaning that their soul is rotting, moving toward entropy and heat-death—they compensate by attempting to control the heat of another. So, a mother might attempt to trap the essence of her teenage daughter and live vicariously off the girl's youth, vitality, and fresh sexual energy. That's also why men who are in their mid-40s (and are approaching male menopause) chase after very young women. It's a death-avoidance mechanism—it's warmth they're seeking. You can spot a heat predator, as they have the eyes that I call "smiling crocodile." They're psychopaths in the making, great talkers who can convince you of anything. When you're watching their flimflam, remember that it's heat they're looking for or money with which to buy it.

Relax your face and look in a mirror. Using the muscles in your cheek, pull up the outer edge of one side of your lips, and you'll see what disdain looks like. It's a low-grade hatred of humanity. Financial predators and rip-off merchants often have mouths that look like they'll try to eat you.

Now, if you ever see someone who has white under his or her irises (between the pupil and the lower eyelid), that's often the sign of a true psychopath. It's known as *sanpaku*. I used to teach my kid and his mates to watch for it in case they were approached by someone who displayed it on the playground. Be careful, however, because sometimes the lower eyelid descends in older people as the muscles of their eyes get weaker. So, they look like they have sanpaku, but it's not psychosis—just the aging process.

If we could walk in the street, I'd show you all of it in several hours, or even less time maybe. But you can teach yourself as I did. No one showed me—I learned by watching. As a person passes, ethereally reach out toward the individual, extending your arm, and grab a small molecule from the center chest area and pull it back toward you quickly. Blank your mind, and don't be overly influenced by what kind of clothes he or she is wearing. As the etheric sample comes to you, ask yourself how it feels. It will take four-tenths of a second for you to receive the response, as that's how long it takes for the brain to decode a reply from the subconscious.

When you go into a restaurant or café, ask yourself, *How does this feel?* The memory of the walls will talk to you. I once had an etheric experience when for a few days, I could see microbes—such as germs on a toilet seat. It was fascinating and a bit spooky. I found myself walking through places sideways, not wanting to touch anything. Like all experiences of the supernatural, my power to see microbes came and went. We know that each experience comes briefly to show us something, and then it leaves. But don't get frustrated, as one day all the powers will find you again. It's the final chapter of remembering. The power is waiting to see whether you'll misuse it. Are you selfless and ready to deliver yourself back to the nostalgia, or do you seek dominance over others?

In the celestial state, you have the ability to step into the ethereal energy of another person. For example, in

my book *Sixth Sense,* I write about moving the etheric—
your subtle body—out of your physical self, turning it to
face you, and then stepping back with it into the physical
body of a person you're talking to (like dropping backward into them). Visiting someone in this way is okay as
long as you're not manipulating or making the person
do things that he or she doesn't want to do. It's a way of
joining and being with an individual, concentrating on
one being. In the end, this is a form of love. When you're
focusing upon a person, you're in the act of loving.

This dropping backward into people's energy is like the
tapping, except they're close to you at the time—not across
the street, say. You're only in there for a few seconds, but
while you're there, you can listen to the sound of their souls.
You can hear and sense who they are and what they're feeling at that instant—it's a snapshot. You have good power!
It lies in and beyond your stored pain . . . some of it's here
right now, and some is only available from time to time,
blipping through when needed.

Forgiving the Dark

You have to forgive the dark and embrace it in order to
get to the light, but it doesn't mean that you must become
evil. It's just that you need to accept it within yourself
and become larger, for to cross the land of the ghouls is a
daunting experience. They use your darkness to attack you,
but once you're bigger than it, you're safe and can travel
back and forth at will without harm. When you finally
step across, you'll also disappear, but don't panic because
you'll return right back again as soon as you wish. It's not
much more than putting your hand up in the Morph and

seeing it melt away, and then bringing it back five minutes later. And there it is, as it always was.

It's only at the very end, decades from now, that all the spiritual warriors and fringe dwellers who have the remembering will each decide. They'll have the option to step across to the other dimension and not return. It's their privilege; they earned it. Or, they can choose to stay here on Earth as teachers, healers, and wise people, but no one knows which world they'll inherit. It may not be the one we know today, as the future world will mostly contain children and some older people and initiates—goodness only knows what will be left.

The scattered Camelots that I discuss in my writing exist so that the children will be safe, and the remembering will flourish for many hundreds of years—maybe even a thousand. Then the knowledge and the Morph will wane, and humans will incarnate here as children of good men and women. But sadly, they won't have the memory of trees, nor will they remember the purpose or the power. And stories of initiates and great healers of this age will enter the mythology of the next one. The story of your simple life and how you made the heroic journey across the great divide may become one of those tales. It will tell of how some people heard the sound of their soul. They began to walk toward it, moving to safety and taking the little children with them.

Come now, my little white goose, and let me tell you about the inner and outer matrix. For like it or not, you'll have to deal with both one day, and without possessing the knowing, you may flounder and be greatly lost.

ESCAPING THE
MATRIX OF CONTROL

In the first *Matrix* film, the character Morpheus talks about "fields upon fields" that form invisible layers of control over humanity. He calls this phenomenon the *Matrix*. What's incredible is that in the five years since we started watching the Morph, we began to see those transdimensional layers that Morpheus refers to—bloody strange that was! We're only now beginning to recognize the enormity of it.

The Inner and Outer Matrix

Humanity is dominated from an unseen world, under the influence of a matrix of unseen entities. But don't let it worry you, for the only way to escape it is to know about it. Ignorance isn't bliss; it's one of the mechanisms of control over us. If you proclaim that humans aren't the most powerful beings here on Earth—that they don't really reign or even have a mind of their own, for the most part—people would think you're nuts, and they'd probably ridicule you, saying it's not possible. Yet that's exactly the truth that's been cleverly hidden from us for tens of thousands of years. When Neo saw it (in the *Matrix* film), he couldn't hack it and threw up.

I'll tell you about the dark forces. And then I'll describe the light ones, and that will cheer you up and give a balanced view. Remember that people's fear of the dark is a deliberate ploy, engineered over the eons to make sure that no one has the courage to confront the opposing force. It's all to prevent an escape to gentleness and the feminine side of things into the arms of the goddess. The idea is for you—too terrified to move—to remain in ignorance inside dogma and yang ideals, so the dark will rule the world forever. People are programmed to react to nonexistent threats. We're fed slime to keep us on edge. Hollywood has helped sell the fear, and in doing so, it has further trapped humanity. To become free, you have to go the other way. You must love and accept the dark and eventually leave the combative, warlike yang that's so prevalent in the global mind-set. In embracing softness and forgiveness, you liberate yourself.

Here's the story, morning glory: There's an inner and an outer matrix of control, and once you know what to look for, you'll see how to fashion an escape from it and its grand fabrications. The New Age and certain religions try to deny the dark, hoping it will go away. But that only allows it to hide evermore in the minds of people and become stronger. Part of our mission here in this life is to expose the transdimensional entities and their mechanism of domination and to teach our brothers and sisters not to be scared anymore. Normally you wouldn't need to know any of this stuff. I could just not mention it, or I could give you the cheesy version: "Rah-rah, living in the light, stick your head in the sand, and everything will be all right." But if I did that, it would mean that I didn't care about you and your soul and whether or not you had the proper knowledge. It would be rather callous of me.

Everything that we now know about the transdimensionals and the dark have come from watching them in the screen of the Morph. How would my frail soul rest if I knew that I sold you a crock and didn't admit to it or tell you what to expect? I have to presume that you're strong, and you'll attempt the journey through the hidden door we've talked about before. To do so, you have to possess the knowing of things, which helps you be less vulnerable. If you're scared of it, you need to realize that it's just a construct in the mechanism of control that was dropped into your mind—nothing more.

Look at it like this: Next to our manipulated world of dishonesty, waffle, and hype and loads of people selling you the illusion of the "up" escalator that takes you the wrong way, there's a forest. And beyond it is heaven. In the forest, there are millions of entities just like on Earth—cute little etheric beings and more gnarly ones who are smelly and nasty but pose no real danger to you. Then there are other beings, like the tiger in our own forests, whom you should be careful to avoid. The tiger is very beautiful and so are you . . . and the dark is beautiful, too. Once you become more mature, you'll be less like a helpless child stuck in this side of the forest, under the control of humans who never want you to escape the system that they profit from.

But if you're going for the great transdimensional journey that our other brothers and sisters and I have taken, you'll have to cross the world of the dark forces that control the inner and outer matrix to arrive at the hidden door. Now I've said that the hidden door isn't a myth, nor is it an allegorical way of talking. It's absolutely real—it frames the gap, so to speak. A quirky way of looking at it is to say that the celestial worlds are surrounded by evil. You must cross the bog of stench before you get to the castle of the Holy Grail. That's the quest of the initiate and the same one that was taken by Perceval and all the would-be seekers since the beginning of time. If anyone tells you differently, they're not being fully honest.

Invisible Spheres of Influence

Here's the background of it all in more depth. In the 15th and 16th centuries, mystics spoke of invisible spheres of influence that surround Earth and humanity. There's a woodcut that shows an initiate of old leaving the spheres of the Earth plane for the other worlds, and French astronomer Camille Flammarion published it in his 1888 book *L'atmosphère: Métérologie Populaire.*

Library of Congress

An initiate leaves the Earth plane and discovers other worlds.

Flammarion lived to be 83 (1842–1925). I find that intriguing . . . maybe he knew something. The sphere theory of medieval times is correct, as humanity really is inside a bubble formed because we live in a physical universe that string theory says is influenced by gravitons—subatomic particles that carry the force of gravity and have to rotate twice in order to return to their initial symmetry. It's the double spin that creates the bubble, or sphere, that we're in. Some particles only have to spin once to achieve their initial state and others have to go two-thirds, but gravitons must spin twice. That's why we have to pass a gravitational anomaly to get out, and I think it's what traps us in this dimension—not allowing an easy escape.

Think of a revolving door at a hotel. You're in the lobby and know that there's a celestial world out in the street. So you enter the door, and it spins very fast—twice—plunking you right back in the lobby, back in 3-D. You never got out! That's why humans are usually stuck. The only way out isn't trying to force your way through. Instead, you have to go sideways along the wall beside the revolving door; there you'll find the hidden entry. Anyway, a long time before that happens, you'll see holes in the wall to reassure you—vortices for you to look down. It's exciting to view these cracks in the matrix. You can peer though the gap and will learn a lot that way.

(*Sidebar:* When you get to the gap and look through, the tip of your nose will go slightly numb. It's the gravitational shift at the door exerting pressure, and it's not unlike the sensation when you put your finger into the vortex formed by the triangle you made with your thumbs and index fingers. The tingling on the fingertip entering that vortex is a faint version of the numb-nose syndrome . . . interesting. Sometimes you'll notice that your fingertips lose feeling for no reason at all, which is also a sign of the Morph. We call it *blister-finger.*)

Okay, back to the hotel and the revolving door. While you're hopelessly trying to get out, there are loads of unseen guards (ghouls) in the lobby making sure you don't escape. Humans are crushed by a hidden deceit that's always there to take us the wrong way or to remind us of our inadequacy. But you can make it! A pal and I traveled through the shadow lands for three and a half years. It's like watching a movie, except you're viewing the screen on the one hand, and you're actually in it at the same time—that's the dual nature of those transcendental worlds. We slipped away under the noses of the ghouls by using the Morph as a lens to instruct us. While moving through, we discovered the secret of the inner and outer matrix of control.

Two Bands of Evil

As I've said, two bands of dark protect the celestial. It's a bit technical, so I'll keep it as simple as possible. Now you might feel it's terrible that you have to travel across this in order to get to the light, but if you think of it from the opposite tangent, it offers a clue. Maybe the ethereal world designed it in that manner, and it likes the fact that two bands of evil guard its dimension. In this way, humans don't arrive before their time, as the dark beats them back. The celestial needs to protect its own pristine nature; the last thing it wants is a human carrying in the ghouls. Unfortunately, our fragile humanity is very polluted. The shadow is dark, and many people have been jumped by entities without realizing it.

Sometimes you'll see beings inside a person's body, living there off the heat—rent free! They're usually between the navel and the pubic bone, and sometimes there's another devilish tenant in the upper body, covering the top of the chest and head. It's a form of alien abduction, except it's not the bug-eyed Grays. They're little demonic beings from the lower worlds, jumping from one person to another. In the Bible, it says that Lucifer fought with the heavenly forces, and he and his dark angels were driven out. While that may be a somewhat simplistic explanation, I feel that it's close to the truth. The celestial guards itself well, and it doesn't want anyone getting there before his or her time. If you wandered in with one of those demonic beings in your belly, all hell would break loose. The number one goal of the ghouls is to reach there, as it offers both warmth and eternity—two things that the ghouls don't have. That's why the secret of the 90-degree world and how to get there has always been hidden in mumbo jumbo, written backward, and couched in rules and jargon that don't really work. It's only now that humans will be allowed in, and that's because the great upheavals are upon us.

(The cure for these demons is very simple: You have to become benevolent, kind, and all-encompassing in your heart. If you do that, they'll leave and jump across to another—*boing!*)

The Outer Matrix

The outer matrix contains all the transdimensional beings who seem to surround us. I use the word *seem* because all of reality is outside of you *and* inside at the same time. This is because your perception of it is only ever an electrical impulse in your brain, so the city street may be outside in the one sense, yet the only way to experience it is inwardly—within yourself.

In the context of the outer matrix, we say that it includes all those ghouls and beings who appear to be outside of us and beyond. For example, there are myriad dark energies that come from a place I call *240 degrees down*. Looking at a compass, it's between south and west, 240 degrees 'round from due north. Stand facing north and place your arms at your sides. Move your left arm about a foot away from your body, and then take it back behind you about a foot and point—that's 240 degrees down. It's a devilish place below and slightly behind you. The beings materialize up through the ground, and that's why you should avoid walking over a drain cover in the street because it leaves you vulnerable to stuff rising from below.

We also found that sitting on the floor is really deadly, as the energies come up and try to penetrate your private parts. They come from a cold 240-degree world seeking heat; and you're fast food for them, life-force food. There's a type of flying etheric bug that we call the *locusts,* and they're mentioned in the book of Revelation. They emit bursts of celestial light like glowworms and fly in the same zigzag way. The locusts come in bunches, 30 to 40 at a time, and sting like crazy if they get you. It's strange to realize that an etheric being can do that, but it can. I saw them every day for five months, but then they disappeared. I don't think that they're something you'll ever have to deal with, as I was bugging them by crossing their lands. I think that's why they tried me! They're tiring, but in the end, they're inadequate—far too slow. We beat them every time. The locusts also don't like chamomile, so we'd fill a bath with half a dozen chamomile tea bags and sit in that for respite. We learned that trick from the Morph. *Easy-peasy-tea-bag-squeezy.*

The UFOs are also from the devil worlds, and although they may appear solid at times, they're in fact entities in the etheric—beings who take on the spaceship look as an identity. It's a type of self-importance, really. They want to appear enigmatic and special. That's why they have a "peekaboo" way of flying about—it adds to the mystery. Now to talk about the UFOs normally invites skepticism and affects one's credibility, but that's what the unseen forces want: disbelief, confusion, ridicule, misinformation, conspiracy theories, and so forth. It's all supposed to sound mad—that's the trick! Trust me, the UFOs are real, and they aren't flying craft or benign space visitors here to help humanity—quite the reverse. They're from inner space and are etheric beings in the Morph. They're real entities, and so are the Grays with the buggy eyes.

I've seen the Grays about half a dozen times. We'd chase them 'round the house with samurai swords. It's a bit crude and unscientific, but we found that it discourages them quite a lot and rather quickly. They don't often encounter humans who aren't scared of them. I've also seen the reptilians once, not a pretty sight. These types of entities are transdimensional beings who are seriously misguided—I call them the devil's air force. They're a part of the outer matrix that secretly forces itself upon humanity in order to exert control. They can talk to the human mind by transferring thoughts, which lead us to conclusions that they want us to accept.

I've come to believe that the beings of the inner and outer matrix politically dominate the world, as they have the influence to furtively steer the minds of leaders and would-be leaders—men and women who revel in power and control. These dark entities are sort of the secret-world government from within because they can speak to the human mind and make people think that what they're hearing are their own thoughts—so they drive legislation, so to speak. That's why governments are so violent, brutal, and cruel. Inner beings control the show, and only someone who has the same ice-cold mind-set makes it to the top. The beings in the outer matrix are like the "squiddies" in the *Matrix* film, a flying army of devilish entities that move around very fast. We're supposed to come to love them in the end. That's the enlightenment of it: They control us with fear, but if we love them, their power is diminished. I'm not all there on the love vibe as yet, but I'm puffing and wheezing and trying as hard as I can.

Some UFOs are saucer shaped but most aren't. Then there are the huge, silent, black flying triangles, such as the one that flew over Phoenix. They're common now. Some UFOs look like flying oil barrels, others are porkpie shaped, and the most familiar variety are just brown blobs, say, three to six feet long and three feet wide. Then there are ones that look like long sticks, and many change shape as you watch, so it's hard to actually describe them. But while they appear solid, they aren't at the same time. They're dark sentient beings who can fly, shape-shift, and morph into many forms. The UFO itself is a being. It's not just a craft, but some people don't realize that yet. If you get fascinated by them as I did, they'll come and find you, and you'll see the Grays in your room. They may try to etherically haul you away, but I'd avoid it if I were you. Even if they don't attempt to grab you, having them around isn't healthy.

(*Sidebar:* The Grays usually only abduct people who have native Indian blood. So if none of your ancestors ever fell in love and had an affair with any native folk, you're fine. Why they only take these people is a huge mystery—no one knows. It seems jolly unfair, but that's the way of it. That's why most of the UFO sightings in the world are over Mexico, as it has a large indigenous population. Weird, eh? If you're a native person, just stay gentle and kind in your heart, for a compassionate feeling is a safe one.)

Sure, you can read a book on the subject of UFOs if you want, but I wouldn't become obsessed. It's quite dangerous. Many UFO researchers get sick and some die young. I believe it's because the beings can hit you with a pulse from a distance. They fire it up your back end if you're male, and they go for the front when attacking females. They're just like the locusts but bigger and nastier.

How I know these things is a funny but sorry tale of misadventure. The story is so out of this world and strange that you'll have difficulty believing me, but you'll find it entertaining and may realize that I couldn't possibly have made it up. Hand on heart, it's 100 percent true. Plus, when this stuff happened, I wasn't on my own—there was another person who came to fight. She witnessed it! Here's the background of it.

There was a time in the Morph when some radiant silver bangles appeared on my wrists. They were hot, and they shone with a godlike light that was very humbling and awe invoking. I didn't know what they were for, but I was beside myself with wonderment just watching them shine. They were bright like the sun. Several days after the bangles appeared, a group of flying blobs and UFO-shaped beings attacked my pal and me. We were in northern Spain at the time. They chased us 60 miles along a freeway, and we eventually hid in the town of Tudela. To cut a long story short, a big transdimensional fight developed in the sky over the center of the town, and it was during then that the bangles lit up and went blisteringly hot. I found that if I flicked my wrist, a red triangle would fly off the left-hand bracelet and travel in a curved path. It would hit one of the blobs or UFO shapes, and the being would shudder and fall from the sky to a lower altitude. It was bloody stupendous to watch! I felt like Captain Marvel.

After a shot went off, I'd drop my arms and there was a subtle *clunk, clunk* feeling as the bangles reloaded and got hot again. I'd walk out into the open from under an arch, and the blobs would dart across the sky heading for me. I'd wait till they got about 100 to 200 yards away and then flick the triangle off my wrist. It would fly as if under some guided system and then *splat*—another blob would go down! I know this sounds nuts, but you have to remember that these are etheric beings—phantoms in the sky, shapes in the mist, if you like. They're just an evolving thought-form of no particular solidity, so there's no debris when they fall from the sky.

Anyway, that battle lasted four hours, and we were subsequently chased a thousand kilometers to a place called La Napoule in France. The chase was scary, as six times trucks crossed the median of the road to take us out—head-on. The next day another battle ensued near Cannes. This time, something like a hundred or more of the unidentified flying blobs engaged in the skirmishes.

Normally when you look up at the blue sky, you think that nothing is there, but the Morph lights up the UFO blobs so that you can see them easily. The first time I ever saw them I was totally shocked. It's so overwhelming. The sky is crowded with UFOs of every shape and size—squadrons of them—and their presence is mostly kept from us. It's a good thing that people can't view them for now, as they'd be terribly frightened if they knew the truth.

In the fracas over La Napoule, I again used the bangles and the red flying triangles. That brawl lasted from nine in the morning until dusk. It was full-on and rather dangerous. Periodically, I'd come out into the open and taunt them to come closer, shouting my worst insults and referring to the sexual proclivities of their mothers (not that they have mothers, as far as I know). Then I'd add insult to injury by dropping my trousers and mooning them—showing 'em my lily-white ass.

The patented "Stuie Wilde white-ass method" is a bit of fun in what's usually a tense situation . . . but I wouldn't recommend it, as I've discovered that it's a bit dangerous. One morning I got out of bed and went out onto a balcony (I was in Bavaria at the time), and there was a brown UFO blob above the pine trees in the distance. When it saw me, it left the treetops and began flying toward me at about 25 miles per hour. I dropped my pajamas and mooned it, but I didn't turn fast enough, and an electronic pulse hit me right up the back end. It hurt like hell! Three days later I got some help from the Morph, and it came out. But it was painful—like a piece of rope with knots and razor blades being extracted from down there. That was one metaphysical experience I could have well done without. Sometimes this transcendental business can make your eyes water!

I still like to moon 'em from time to time—they're only misguided street trash that learned to fly—but I'm way more careful now. Nobody gets a free run in this matrix game, plus my bangles disappeared one day, and for five years I didn't see them. Then one night I woke up at 3 A.M. and my wrist was prickling. A bangle popped into view; it just flashed on and off periodically for about five minutes. I thought to myself that I've had enough of this UFO rubbish and it was time to pull their membership card off the rack (*delete, forced quit*)!

"Dream on, Stuie, dream on!" There are billions of them. It would be like saying that you wanted to rid the world of fleas. But I have this childlike ability to attempt the impossible, like when your kid jumps off the garden wall wearing a Batman outfit! The weird thing is that sometimes when I tried for the unattainable, I got it. On other occasions I didn't get all of it, I just got some; and the rest of the time I broke my bloody leg—metaphorically speaking. I don't know if you agree, but I feel that being slightly zany and trying for impossible things is better than watching the telly and daydreaming about 33 ways of pushing your mother-in-law into the canal in the dead of night . . . pleasing as those meditations might be at times.

In conclusion, the blobs and the UFOs are part of an immense spiritual evolution in the outer matrix that feeds off humans attempting to control what happens here. There are more of them than there are of us humans—we're in the minority here, strange to say. One day it will all come out in the wash; meanwhile, they impose a psychological agenda on us, which I consider evil. They thrive off of human fear, so they manipulate systems to create it. Don't buy the fear; it's rubbish. Be brave and go the other way because it's all a sham. If you see a flying object, give it the middle-finger salute, as that's the preferred welcome as laid out in the *Stuie Wilde Annals of This and That.*

In the Morph, we've seen all sorts of other etheric entities, such as big black spiders that hover over the heart chakra when you sleep and little flying bugs that look like midgets. They seem to thrive on the outside of our energy field—hovering in the air, about a foot away. They have tiny spindly legs that pump up and down furiously. In a spooky kind of way, they're quite sweet, but we'll talk more about the bugs later.

It might all sound jolly unlikely—etheric beings in a parallel evolution, blipping in and out of this one—but you may be familiar with the work of researcher Jose Escamilla, who has photographed an etheric being that he calls the *flying rod.* The flying rods are anywhere from a few inches long to 50 feet in length. Some have fins that oscillate along their translucent etheric bodies, rushing through the air at speeds of hundreds of miles an hour, and they can also exist underwater. They've probably always been here in the outer matrix.

Escamilla discovered the flying rods by accident when his video camera was left on one day. While editing the film, he noticed strange objects zip into view, turn, and then fly out again, all in the space of a few frames. He's since filmed hundreds of them. In one clip that I saw, there are two people talking when a rod flies into the scene at about waist height, moves 'round them, and then flies out of the shot. What are flying rods? No one knows, least of all Escamilla. They're beings in the fields upon fields that Morpheus describes. (Jose is a really cool, innovative researcher. You can find his work on **www. roswellrods.com**, or look him up in a search engine.)

Some of the rods are saddle shaped, which is interesting because the universe is also shaped that way. It looks exactly like a Pringles chip—according to the Morph, anyway. Here's a photo of a saddle-shaped one.

Dann Nelson

A flying rod in Brazil.

The point here is that our world is controlled by beings from an unseen realm: This is *their* world. The idea that it's *our* world is a delusion of grandeur that keeps the human ego happy, but it isn't metaphysically or transcendentally correct. The field that sustains the beings in the outer matrix has become stronger because its first heat source is electricity; and it's been empowered by the electrification of the world and the global grid system, just as the ego's ivory tower is fueled by the bioelectricity of the mind—they're very similar. With the advent of microwave towers that run mobile-phone systems, the ghouls of the outer matrix had a new power source, so they increased exponentially. It's heat that the ghouls desire. Remember that they come from a cold world—240 degrees down is bleak and freezing, and that's why they gather like crows on electrical sources.

Go outside at dusk and take a look. Use your side vision, as I described earlier, and you'll see the dark entities on the wires or hovering around the tops of cellphone towers. You'll observe them oscillating, moving very fast, and warming themselves prior to heading off again. Now don't panic! I'll show you how we managed and even thrived after the world of the ghouls. There are good beings who come from the hidden doorway and are fighting their way into here. But this matrix stuff is something you need to know, especially if you want to move across the dimensions to a Camelot world of the Holy Grail and become part of a celestial evolution here on Earth.

The Beings of the Inner Matrix

The dark forces of the inner matrix are different from the flying etheric beings of the outer one. In many ways, the inner matrix is more deadly because it's inside your mind, lodged in the collective unconscious of humanity. It's made up of thoughts that are layered over society like a net or blanket—it's very real. It also forms an invisible control, a consensus, that's similar to the guards in the lobby, really. The inner matrix contains our darkness and the individuals who died but are still evil and nasty. If you've ever begun to meditate and have seen faces quickly appear in front of you, you've seen the place I'm describing. I call those images *flashy faces,* and you pass those spirits on your way inward toward the celestial. I always imagine that their world is placed around us like the rings of Saturn, strengthening around the minds of people with evil tendencies.

Those beings are powerful and angry, and like those of the outer matrix, they can secretly communicate with your mind. So they attack psychologically because they can play on your weaknesses and manipulate your memories to cause you to feel sadness, pain, remorse, or guilt. Mainly they organize humanity to conform, and they don't want you to redeem yourself because they damned themselves to darkness and are now stuck. The idea that you'll escape their control makes them go berserk. If you think differently or try to challenge the norm, the beings of the inner matrix will attack. They can make you rather depressed and sick, and they're hard to beat off—penetrating you deeply and testing your limits all the way.

Rudolf Steiner (the great Austrian mystic of the early 1900s) had a concept he called the Guardian of the Threshold, a force of evil that blocks the doorway. It was said that the guardian was the keeper of your greatest weakness; in order to get through, you had to face it. I reckon that the entities of the inner matrix are the guardians in one form or another.

The beings of the outer matrix are anal and stupid for the most part, but the inner ones are very clever and use guile to empower their dark realm. They bring forth doubt, guilt, and shame—anything to disrupt your balance. It doesn't matter to them if it takes decades because they have lots of time. They know that if they plug away, they might get you in the end; and if they can't trap you with guilt or fear, they sometimes try to lure you with self-importance. They sell the idea that you're spiritually special, chosen—elevated above others. In this way, they abduct people to their elitist world, and vulnerable humans strut about, believing they're privileged and saved.

Generally you see the beings of the outer matrix, such as the flying rods, with your eyes open and see those of the inner matrix with them shut. They appear in your visions as images of human faces, albeit ugly ones, and even if you haven't seen them, you can feel their influence. It's a bad vibe, like when you walk into a bar, for example, and instantly know it's all wrong—it's ghoul infested. The trick is to learn to trust your feelings and walk out.

The forces of the inner matrix are discarnate entities, like floating human minds. They can move around the planet at will, but only within the area that Jung called the collective unconscious. All of them seem human to us. It's impossible to tell whether they're people who have died and passed over, or if they're mirror-world existences of humans who are still alive right now. I've seen individuals in the mirror-world whom I know are still living on Earth, and I've also seen others there who have passed on. So I would say that the spirits of the dead as well as the subconscious minds of the six billion people who are alive today populate the inner matrix. These beings don't manifest outside of the human mind (as far as we know), but sometimes they take control of it in the form of a psychological possession. Then you would see zombies, the living dead, but that's rare, as you usually only see the beings of the inner matrix in your mind's eye. They can't really hurt you physically, but they exert a type of gravity on your emotions and feelings and can also appear in your dreams.

Using the *Matrix* film as an analogy, we could say that Zion is the world of humans, and the squiddies are the flying ghouls and etheric spirits in the outer matrix. Agent Smith and his anal cohorts—so devoid of warmth—are the discarnate beings of the inner matrix. Since these sentient programs reside in the human mind, they can transform into anyone, just as Smith morphs into other people. The movie is very accurate in its metaphysical analogy. If you haven't seen it, you might want to pick it up from the video shop.

The way to stay safe from the inner matrix is to keep your spirits up at all times and never let things get you down for long. You have to offer yourself forgiveness for any transgressions, and don't dwell on them. Incorporate your faults or errors and vow to do better in the future, for if the beings of the inner matrix see your insecurity come up from within, they fly across the collective unconscious in seconds to strike you emotionally, hoping to push you to rack and ruin. They want you as one of their own. The human subconscious isn't just a collection of ideas; it's where all of our hidden thoughts reside. It's a part of our identity, and what I don't think Jung realized was that it's a place—a dimension where spirits evolve.

I discovered all this wild and wonderful stuff in the early days when I first saw the outer matrix as a honeycomb pattern that's all around us—it's dome shaped, sort of like being inside a net. I wondered how on earth I'd ever get out of it. By then I had failed miserably with the mirrored-cage idea. A bit later on I started to see little blips of blue light that seemed to be shining through the matrix from beyond. They were just pinpricks at first, but after a couple of years, I noticed that a darker patch appeared around them, as if the honeycomb was less strong—not broken necessarily, but slightly darker looking. So one day I decided to will myself toward the spot where the matrix seemed weakened, and I found myself beyond the net, in a celestial world.

After that all hell broke loose, as the beings of the outer and inner matrix came 'round like gangbusters. One of the human drones escaped! When you pop out through the net, you can pick any spot that seems to be offered, but when you come back into 3-D, it seems to me that you reenter through the hole you exited from. So they're aware of where you're going to be and they wait. This makes the journey back pure agony, for by now the ghouls know who you are and exactly where to find you. You'll be surrounded for a long time. After the Morph arrived in the spring of 2001, it took me three months to learn my way out of the matrix and three and a half years to lose the ghouls that followed me back. But you don't have to worry about that because now there are ways out without the dark beings tormenting would-be escapologists. Covered pathways are now being built.

I went to the matrix early with the help of just one person (she was very brave, top-notch). We had to forage through and work it out by trial and error, but I discovered that the ghouls can make you sad and can *ping* you with energy hits that knock you about a bit. It won't kill you, and as long as you're strong and have begun to resolve your shadow, you'll be able to endure it. If you want to transcend and redeem yourself, you must travel through the inner matrix of the ghouls because they are your shadow-self internally manifested. Only living saints might avoid them, but then again, I don't know if the evil beings would torment them all the more just because they're thoroughly good.

This brings us back neatly to the idea of the authentic you, because the mirror-self is the real you and the intellect and ego are not—they're just a concoction of ideas and opinions, programs that you inherited from the matrix. The mirror-self is your true identity: It's what you silently trust and feel about life, not what you pretend to believe. Sometimes known as the doppelganger, it can operate in the mirror-world without permission from your waking mind, as if your subconscious goes walkabout without your intellect having a say in what it's doing or where it's heading. Your mirror-self operates 24/7 regardless of whether you're awake or sleeping.

It's also possible that the authentic you may be quite evil and that's okay, as it's part of your evolution. First you observe it and then decide whether or not to change. Maybe you're an aspect of the prince or princess of darkness—just realizing that and admitting to it is a huge step forward. Most people deny any knowledge of it, which leaves them vulnerable to the ghouls because the insistence on their perfection is childlike and unsophisticated. The only safety is to look at the dark, see its beauty, forgive it, and transmute it.

A Strange and Powerful Idea

There's enormous power inside your darkness; and with it you can resolve the authentic you, fusing it to the energy of the physical, intellectual, and emotional levels that you're operating with here on Earth. It's a strange and powerful idea that you can use to unlock the matrix and escape. The light doesn't resist, for it's not in its nature to fight, and anyway, down here in our world the light is very weak compared with the dark. Don't forget that this is the kingdom of evil forces. In order to get out of this etheric dungeon, you must use your own darkness to carry you across. It's the only way to overcome the dark . . . hold that idea for a sec.

The inner you, the mirror-world you, is authentic. It's the missing part of yourself, like a twin who was separated at birth. If you have a deep, inner disquiet that something is lacking in life (many do), what's lost is your dark brother or sister. It will probably be rather nasty, and it may be roaming around the mirror-world looking for people to feed off of or to profit from—just as the ghouls at 240 degrees down attempt to come up from below to prey upon humans. The point is that you can never escape unless you bond with it, the other half. It's massively powerful compared with the human you, as it doesn't have the same vulnerabilities and confusion. In the mirror-world it can see what it is—be it good, bad, or ugly—so it has a certainty inside that you don't have. That knowledge gives you the power to step forward and confront the ghouls and fight them off. It's a big force and few are aware of it.

What you are here in your waking state is just a mask that you present to the world as part of a social game that suits your agenda. You might play the good person or decent mother, but the reality deep inside may be that you're in fact a little devil—an elitist, miser, manipulator, or racist mafioso who will harm others in a flash. This is the essence of the journey beyond transcendence: You see it all as one and decide to make your symmetry or the imprint of your life beautiful, not ugly. And the first place of real power is to admit that you're the prince of darkness or an evil witch who is full of him- or herself. Going for the dark (what I call *endarkenment*) and not being scared of it is the secret to everything.

When I tell people that they have to go the other way and embrace endarkenment, they get edgy or don't believe me, but the darkness is, in effect, not really dark at all. It's just stored pain, ancient torment—the sins that you inherited from hundreds of years ago, down through your family history. There's a heroic beauty there if you can resolve it. Then you can save others from going the wrong way, and maybe they don't have to go through the cluster from their ancestors, as you broke it for them. While the power of ancient suffering may have hurt at the time, it will now turn and empower you. It's your shield across the ghoul lands, especially once you love your dark inner brother or sister and you're no longer afraid. Your stored pain is beautiful. Start to tell yourself that it was all just a learned response, a digital, mathematical karma you inherited—a spiritual lesson. You know that you can transform it from a tormentor to a guard who works on your behalf.

The Temptation of Christ

Here's something that I found rather fascinating. When Jesus was fasting out in the desert, the dark came to visit him three times. And on each occasion, he denied it. But if you read the text, all that the devil wanted was a bit of love and acceptance—nothing more. The devil said, "All I want is for you to call me your brother." (So the devil was going through his own rejection trip—a bit of stored pain—yet Jesus spurned him.) Jesus thought that the dark was outside of him, not a part of himself or his shadow and psychology. But it wasn't; it was always inside, within the inner matrix, as Jesus was in the matrix—all humans are.

Because Jesus couldn't accept his dark (and love and care for it by making it right and whole again), he was left unprotected. He never had its power to defend against an even bigger darkness, which was the church elders plotting to kill him. Jesus was suckered into a shadow play because he thought he was better than the temple people, so he beat up on the money changers there. You have to remember that Jesus was poor and came from an alternative group of hippies who weren't well-off or high up the social ladder. He got angry at the wealth and injustice of the temple. You see, he could have embraced his ancient pain of rejection and poverty and just walked away, leaving the merchants to be merchants, but in attacking the *bureau de change* department, he highlighted the fact that he considered himself white and right. He wanted to take on the darkness of the hierarchies that, in his view, weren't as righteous and good as he was. The problem was that he confronted very powerful forces that controlled all of Jewish life.

Ya man didn't really have the power to pull it off . . . now did he? He couldn't destroy them, and it was daft to take them on. He needed his "little brother" (his darkness) with him. You can't fight the dark with the light, but Jesus rejected the dark when he said to the devil in the desert, "Get behind me, Satan!" Jesus was all love and compassion, yet he couldn't offer affection and forgiveness for the dark, his little brother. But Jesus's attitude was a bit harsh, and then his dark brother said, "I will give you everything if you kneel and worship me," meaning that in the humility of acceptance and the fusion of dark and light, there's transcendence. But JC wouldn't have it and didn't take the opportunity offered to him.

If Jesus had gone forth into the world with his devilish brother out in front as his shield, he might have made it and perhaps overthrown the temple priests and established the new Jewish order that he so desperately wanted—one that didn't discriminate against the poor. His heart was in the right place, but he got it all 'round backward. He could have possibly broken the matrix and beaten the ghouls, but he didn't see it, and that's why he called out on the cross asking, "Why have you forsaken me?" We've all done the same thing in the dead of night when we felt abandoned and confused. His father (the light) didn't forsake him; it was Jesus who abandoned himself, for the light can't come down through the hidden door and beat away the ghouls of the inner and outer matrix. If it could, it would have already done so a million years ago. Nor can it defeat the darkness. Only the dark can defend you against the dark—strange but true. Jesus might have been the Son of God, but he wasn't infallible, and he seemed to make mistakes like we all do—never mind . . . next time.

Nostradamus and the Bible talk of the anti-Christ, a tyrant who rises to destroy the Western world and bring down Christianity. But this being could just be formed from Dirac's antiparticles, which you'll remember are just portions of a different electrical polarity. In other words, the anti-Christ could be Jesus's shadow-self in the mirror-world. It's like saying the human shadow will rise up and annihilate all of life. If you watch the antics of the 9/11 story and all the nonsense going on in the Middle East, you can observe the shadow of humanity and see that the anti-Christ is already creeping out of its hiding place (which, of course, is inside our collective mind). Like the little darkness that Jesus wouldn't acknowledge, our unified devils within will cause a lot of mayhem and fuss until we agree to look at them, forgive, and tend to their needs.

The primary want is to be recognized and made whole. The dark desires redemption and absolution, as you and I do, and seeks to move away from the cold toward the heat. In the ecology of the soul, you're not allowed to leave without the darkness, as the last thing that's needed is billions of bits of unclaimed psychological sewage in the celestial lost-and-found department. That collective dark has to be transmuted before it's carried out. This strange idea isn't scary—in fact, it's very beautiful. The anti-you, mirror-world you, and shadow-you are all the same; embracing that grants you the power to defend yourself. If you ponder it for a while, you'll become excited, for you'll know that the splinter in your mind is about to be removed. The resolved human is a whole being, delivered and redeemed and finally made well.

Consider this: The ghoulish entities of the inner matrix know the truth of you, and they'll tear at your soul and drag you about like a rag doll until you get it. Living in the light is very nice, and you certainly want to be compassionate, but you also have to be a dark individual, one who understands the secret of it all. Anything else is untrue and doomed to failure—it's a trick and it's backward. That's the knowledge of the power that I'm talking about: fusing your stored pain to form the authentic you. In that suffering is a massive explosion of energy that delivers a new liberation. It's your shield. Once you love it, embrace it, and make it your brother (or your little sister), it will go out ahead to protect you, making you whole.

All of the rubbish about the shadow and the scary stuff you've been told was dished out to you like boiled cabbage at a school cafeteria. It was placed there to ensure that the secret to everything would be kept, and you'd be paralyzed by fear and stay trapped in the matrix forever. Here's a point to think about. After a disaster such as 9/11, the relatives of the victims are on television saying what marvelous people the deceased were: good fathers, wonderful mothers—you'd imagine that no one had any faults. They were all Mr. Nice Guys (or Ms. Goody Two-shoes), perfectly white people with no protection at all. The true bastards probably missed the event, or they got out of the building.

It's a shadow thing; too much Mr. Nice Guy can be dangerous to your health, for it's set in the hard shell of denial. You see, without your little dark sibling, you'll be crucified throughout your life because you're lacking protection, knowing, and real power. You're destined to suffer the sadness of rejection or disease that comes from cold cells and fall into futile despair while waiting end-lessly for the light to rescue you—and it never comes. I'm sure you know precisely what I mean. The light can entice you to make the journey, but it can't come and get you.

Shadow Impulses

Here's a shadow exercise so that you can test your-self. Sit at a bar or in a restaurant (anywhere people hang out to relax, have a drink, and watch others come and go), blank your mind, and pay attention as the inner you responds to the stimulus of the individuals walking through the door. Clear your thoughts and notice where your mind goes and the kinds of things you concentrate on when you allow your subconscious impulses to come forward. See what conclusions you reach about others, and observe how your intellect translates those pulses into a story—one that you tell yourself about a person whom you have your eye on. In effect, you're watching while also noticing what's coming from within you.

Your inner self will go for people's stored pain—especially anything that looks similar to your own suffering—so be mindful, as it judges those individuals without knowing anything about them. You may silently scowl or growl if a person comes in whom you dislike. Maybe they're wearing clothes you don't agree with, and that brings forth a childhood fear of the boogeyman or the hurt of an early rejection. You negate the person you're looking at because you've experienced the same feeling as a child.

If a fat older man arrives arm in arm with a pretty young girl in a short skirt, you may react by deciding that he's a dirty old man and she's a little gold digger or a slut. Of course, you don't know the facts—he could be her uncle! In examining the inner you, you see how it forms conclusions from its data bank of stored pain. If you're a man, you might be jealous that the girl isn't with you. She then represents all the women who have ever turned you down, which you project as negative energy toward her and the old man walking in the door. He may be the sweetest, kindest gent in the world, but you'll wallpaper him in your bitterness, and that's how the energy of the subconscious can affect your imprint on the world. Life is painted silently by the throb of your former experiences—often the pulse of a silent malediction.

Soon you'll see if you're human and warm in your heart . . . or are you just a cold reptilian predator of humanity—an Agent Smith in disguise? As the woman in the red dress came through the door, did you look at the flowers she was carrying, or was your attention pulled to her sexuality? And of course, the girl in the short skirt we just talked about may well be responding to her impulses and urges. Maybe she's using sex to entice people, or she's just seeking attention. Perhaps it's a money thing, and she requires admirers to help pay for her to have a good time. But the ones who lust after her are in a shadow play as stalkers and probably don't respect her as a woman or care for her soul—they just want her to submit to them. On the other hand, she might be pure and in love with her boyfriend, and she put on the short skirt because she likes it, it gives her confidence, and she feels pretty wearing it.

There are endless factors that make up our collective inner madness. Sometimes the stored pain manifests as inverted snobbery, which is when individuals who are socially or economically disadvantaged feel better or more special than rich people and hate high achievers. It's the angry revolutionary who detests the upper class because he or she isn't included in it. It's the Communist proletariat rising up to assassinate the czar because they secretly love and want to be more like their leader. Inverted snobbery is the feeling of being superior to the systems or the people who reject you. It's common in churches and spiritual groups. But it's weird because it's all backward—the folks and the things that you pretend to hate are really those hidden parts you're secretly infatuated with or desire.

Love is a form of concentration, and romance is focusing on an individual to the exclusion of others. To detest someone, you must also direct your mind to the person, projecting thoughts toward him or her. Usually the one you abhor has something you admire or want—something that will help you understand your stored pain. Funny, eh? Now you might say, "Listen up, Stuie bubba, what do I need all this malarkey for? I'd like to stay up on the light end of things and just live in the dippy-do-lally of all that . . ." and I'd answer, "Do as you want!"

You are a fallen angel and so am I. There's no reason to stand up if you don't want to, but almost all of your power is locked in the ancient pain. In fact, it's not dark— it's your light, and you have to harness the energy of it in order to make the crossing. That's not to say that you must embrace any new evil or take to satanic ways; it's just that you need to enter into the humility of knowing the dark. Living in the light is fine as long as it's not part of the arrogance of denial. Once you have your darkness to defend you, the ghouls back off, but without it, you're a hamburger on the griddle to them.

Understanding the imprint you give off helps you realize why people react to you. Of course, they respond to your benevolence as well as your hidden darkness, but maybe you're trying to figure out why opportunities elude you. Why do people silently say no without your necessarily knowing why they're rejecting you? If you repel them, why is that so? Do you know? Perhaps you scare them with your unresolved anguish, or maybe your weakness irritates them and you're too needy. It's a shadow trait to lean on others for financial and emotional support. It's possible that you're too slimy and the hidden predator is leaking out. Are you sneaky and loose with the truth, so people instantly distrust you? They might think you're after their money . . . are they right?

Maybe there's a host of inner ghouls following you about, riding your unresolved pain and ready to jump across from you to others. Perhaps people sense that and back away, fearing for their safety. Some individuals believe in bad luck or that they're accident-prone, but that's the simplistic explanation—mostly they're ghoul-tormented. They need to be rescued from the problem of only being half a person. While darkness hides to infest your mind, it's a victory for those energies of the inner matrix that want you depressed, miserable, and bitter. They want you as both the predator and controller on the one hand, and the victim and prisoner on the other. They want everyone to hurt each other as much as possible and fail just as they have.

If it all sounds extraordinary and unlikely, ask yourself this poignant question: *Have I ever heard of another person's misfortune or read in the paper about someone falling from grace and found that I was silently pleased?* It's hard to admit, but we all do it sometimes. Does the pain of others give you a sense of power and well-being; do you derive comfort from it? If so, it's an aspect of your dark, in the sense that it's expressing a need to enhance the light. The suffering and failure of others allows for your light to feel more special, cleaner, and brighter. Sometimes the pain of others falling down leaves you with the illusion of moving up—it's part of the interplay of light and dark. The ghouls are no different, because they're an extension of us. Now here's a bit more on setting yourself free and beating the matrix.

Defending Yourself Well in the Matrix

The first defense, of course, is to have strong sentiments that affirm your wish to go in the opposite direction toward goodness and the feminine spirit. It starts with constructing a new impression of your etheric energy: the act of becoming aware. So if you sat in a bar observing people and you imprinted everything as beautiful, you would see each person with a soft eye—that's your first defense. Once your shadow-self is made special, it becomes calm and will accept everyone (saints and sinners) and will cause less trouble. No one is outside of and separate from you; eternally they're all inside. The fact that you're watching and reacting means their anguish is similar to yours, and realizing that, you become benevolent and kind in the silence of your mind. The matrix around you transforms because the memory of your pain changes.

As you're viewing people, start by setting up the coordinates in your mind so that the power of the ghouls that have just come through the barroom door won't jump on you and follow you home. When you see the girl in the short skirt, silently project kindness in your mind's eye, sending her love and noticing how bright and flowery she looks. Maybe you take a mental image of a small posy of purple lavender and place it in her heart to make up for the lousy thoughts you had a minute before. And the dirty old man you first saw melts away, and now you see his strength and the wisdom in the lines of his face. You think that his young female companion is lucky to have a good friend like him, and so forth.

It that way you may also remember some good qualities of your father, such as how hard he worked to provide for the family, and perhaps recognize how you judged him harshly. Maybe you no longer focus on what went wrong, for you see that it's all set in a construct that none of us can completely comprehend—it's black, white, and gray. Even the most wicked of us frail creatures have goodness someplace deep within, and if they don't exhibit it right now, never mind because you didn't arrive here perfect either. You came to learn about yourself, but if you stand over others or act as their judge and jury, that's a ghoulish projection of evil. You never know what trials and tribulations they've been through. The way to stay safe is to disconnect.

Here's an imprint thing from the Morph that highlights what I'm saying. As we've discussed, some ghouls in the matrix are like little bugs that usually hover at the outer edge of your etheric, feeding off your energy at night. I try to grab them with my hands like swatting a fly, but you can only see them when your mind is almost asleep in a deep delta brain pattern (which is one to four cycles per second—that's just as you first wake up). In that drowsy state, it's very hard to operate your limbs quickly, and often I find that my arms are tangled in the sheets of the bed, preventing any quick moves. When you're roused, the etheric insects sense it and run away, usually dematerializing through the ceiling of the room you're in. Sometimes the spiders are as wide as your hand, and they hover a foot or so from your face while you're sleeping. They're black, with nasty spindly legs that pump up and down energetically. They're not much fun! On a scale of one to ten, I'd say they're close to zero—not pretty.

In the beginning, I only saw the etheric bugs once every two to three months, so they didn't bother me much. (Although I was visited by a type of etheric midget that was a bit daunting—they swarm toward you in bunches of 30 to 40, usually descending from the ceiling.) Then recently I started to see them every day, first at night when I fell asleep and again in the morning. They troubled me a lot because they feel intrusive. I grabbed one of the spiders once, and when I opened my hand expecting to see a dead bug, I saw instead what looked like a little piece of burned paper. The thing was no longer spider shaped, and it floated off my hand and up through the ceiling. Grabbing the bugs isn't really the answer, though, so I started to breathe love at them instead, which was much better. Sometimes the spiders are red and resemble furry golf balls with legs, suspended in midair. I watched one cross the room toward me, so I shot it a squirt of the love vibe and it immediately halted.

Over a few weeks I noticed something strange: Anytime I was emotionally disturbed or even slightly frustrated about something, the etheric bug population increased exponentially. They seem to feed off our negative emotions—maybe it offers them extra heat. I started to do a short process where I'd breathe love to them, humanity, and individuals who might have upset me. I did that just before going to sleep, and I noticed that the number of bugs decreased dramatically and they finally went away. But after a few days when I got lazy on the love-love routine, they came back.

It all goes back to the resonance of your soul. When you're emotional or antagonistic, your soul goes brown and dirty, and you pull etheric beings to you much like the bacteria that live off garbage. In trying to understand the bugs, I asked a question of my higher mind, and one morning when I woke up, I saw a vision of two dozen or so little pink hearts floating toward me. That's when I realized that even small upsets affect your energy because they allow for more intrusion from the beings in the matrix. I found all that rather interesting. The etheric insects aren't so unusual, for there are tiny bugs in real life that live in your eyebrows—under a microscope, they look like little dinosaurs, and there's nothing you can do about them. Very little of your weight is flesh; most of the human body is bacteria. We're a bag of germs that's wrapped in skin . . . no wonder it all feels a bit weird.

Here's an extra tip: Never use those old-fashioned electric blankets. The energy is food for the ghouls, and they're attracted to it. Anyway, it's dangerous to be too close to electricity, as it gives off an alpha particle that travels though your body, turning healthy cells into dangerous ones. That's the reason why people who live near electrical towers are more susceptible to leukemia and other diseases of cell mutation. It's also very bad for children.

The Linden Points

In Teutonic legend, Siegfried slayed a dragon and then bathed in its blood. In the brutality of that act, he sought to protect himself using the very essence of the dragon—its blood—as his shield. It's the beast's darkness defending Siegfried and granting him immortality. But while he was washing in it, a leaf from a linden tree fell onto his back, so a part of his body wasn't touched by the blood and didn't receive its powers.

We discovered that the mythology is essentially correct. There are, in fact, two key spots on your back where you're vulnerable, and you should learn to protect them because they're where the ghouls will try to strike. When they hit one or more of the points, it feels like a sharp skewer in your back. The unprotected areas are on either side of the spine, about halfway up the shoulder blade.

Have a mate apply pressure in the area until you find their exact location—they usually ache a bit when pressed.

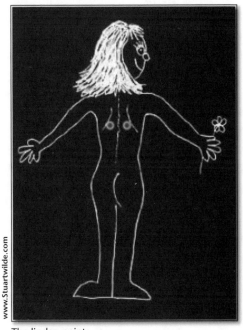

www.Stuartwilde.com

The linden points.

We call these areas the linden points, and it's useful to know about them. You may notice when you're out and about that energy from others jumps across the street and strikes you. When the Morph was full-on between 2001 and late 2004, I got hit about 20 times a day. If this happens to you, visualize it as a skewer and attempt to remove it: Reach behind—and even though you can't see it—try to grab it and pull it out. Afterward you can dress the spot with a little dab of tea-tree oil. The ghouls hate it, and we also found that they don't like the Italian liqueur Fernet Branca because it's very bitter. (The German version of it is Jägermeister.) You can use this if tea-tree oil isn't available.

The linden points aren't related to your shadow work or resolving stored pain, but if you learn to protect them, you'll be healthier and less vulnerable to attack. Although the ghouls will try to penetrate you over and over, you'll find that in time they'll be less effective—so there's a light at the end of it all. But remember this: Just as the evil Agent Smith in the *Matrix* film could morph into anyone to mount an assault on Neo or the others, so can the ghouls. They can bounce off any human in the street, and of course, there are millions of people who have been abducted without ever knowing it. The ghouls have allies everywhere! The fewer ghoul-infested individuals you hang out with the better, and it also helps to avoid places that are swarming with them.

Isn't it interesting that the writers of ancient wisdom and the Siegfried myth were aware of the vulnerable place on our backs? I always thought that there were people on Earth who understood much of this etheric stuff long before we rediscovered it—I'd love to know what other secrets they uncovered.

More Etheric Protection

Next defense: The ghouls are drawn to anything that's dirty, messy, vile, or humanly degrading, so they cling to dust, clutter, and disorder, as well as to dark sentiments (as I've mentioned). They're attracted to dysfunction and the heat of pornography and emotional outbursts, such as fear and power trips, violence, drug abuse, S and M, and torture. In seeking heat, they go for your private parts. Ghouls are like bacteria; their existence depends on constantly feeding off of us. That's why keeping clean becomes part of your protection—it's vital. They're especially attracted to blood, so ladies on their moon should be careful to stay very clean. When in the bathroom, you might want to make sure that you wash thoroughly, and if you can't shower, use a wet sheet of tissue instead. What you're trying to do is to be cleaner than other people so the ghouls go for them—not you. Keeping your clothes spotless and fresh helps to that end.

Now I don't want to preach, but I ought to mention that if you use marijuana, you leave yourself open to the ghouls. It tears at your etheric, breaking down your protection, and the dark beings play to the paranoia that it sets up. The THC (tetrahydrocannabinol) oil in pot is stored in your brain, where it interferes with neurological synapses. If you must have it, then try to limit it to one joint a week as a special treat—not every day. Marijuana is a ghoul's birthday banquet—they love it! If there are people around you who smoke pot, try your best to avoid them. The area is bound to be infested, and entities can easily jump across a room (I've seen it many times). You don't want to judge others, but you do need to protect yourself and walk away if possible. I'm trying not to wag my finger here—if you want to use it, do what you like, but it's a bit deadly to your long-term metaphysical future. If you're a habitual pot smoker, you don't have much of a chance (in this lifetime anyway) of getting out of the matrix. You'll have to stay here and get stoned . . . it could be worse.

The downside is that pot opens you up, and in that state, the ghouls will fill your head with nonsense. They'll take you for a ride up the primrose path, and you'll get a lot of misinformation and warped ideas that may plunge you into inactivity and disappointment. Pot is an avoidance mechanism, a sad man's medicine, and it's also a terrible trap because the oil is poisonous. There's no known way of getting it out of the brain, and it carries you toward psychosis over a long period of time. The really scary part is that it allows for abduction. That's why pot smokers are vulnerable—not just because their souls and their etheric are brown and weakened—but also because the ghouls capture them.

In the late '80s and early '90s, several books came out about alien abduction. People reported being hauled off against their will by the Grays in the middle of the night. It's very real and nasty, but it only represents the tip of the iceberg. Ghoul abduction is subtle and quite common, and it's done in secret, so society knows little about it. The beings of the inner matrix worm their way into your mind so that they can start to feed your impulses, offering you ideas that aren't far from what you already believe. Because what they're imparting isn't totally unacceptable, you come to agree bit by bit and eventually begin to lean toward them without realizing it—and it grows.

For example, sex addicts often drift into the extreme, verging on abuse. That's the effect of the ghouls driving the bus. Pornography is the same because it's a lust for control—deep inside, this trait is the desire for someone to submit to your will. Pedophilia is another demonic characteristic; predators stalk children because they feel powerless. Both of these are power trips in the sense that they're manifestations of the slave master's mind. That's why child sexual abuse has reached epidemic proportions in Africa, as millions of people there have no economic status and thus, no voice or influence. All of this dark stuff is an open door for the ghouls to walk into your heart and set up shop.

Ghoul abduction is widespread, and millions more will fall victim to them, to a lesser or greater degree. They're clever—brilliantly devilish—because they know how to talk to your weaknesses. There are 44 main ways that the ghouls can enter your mind and energy, whisking you off to be a prisoner in their world. This isn't a topic that we should enter into deeply here, as it's truly vile and not fun to discuss. If I revealed it all, you might become terrified—and that in itself is an invitation. Suffice it to say that any action, feeling, or thought seeking to degrade or misuse others carries you in the mirror-world to the gates of hell. Sexism, racism, hatred, violence, emotional abuse, control trips, and dishonesty will get you closer there—you get my idea. If you drift toward the hellish state in the mirror-world, the loop effect brings you back and the dark impulses grow here in this world. Feeding your mirror-self with more darkness will transport you down the slippery path even farther. Remember that the afterlife is now—if you're currently at the gates of hell in the inner world, that's where you'll find yourself if you suddenly died.

Sometimes it's bloody difficult to get people out of trouble, as the loop is self-enforcing. Rescuing individuals who have been abducted by entities in the shadow world is treacherous because the part of them that has been captured (that is, possessed) attacks the rescuer, who's seen as a threat to the very existence of the person's darkness. I used to have a trait in me that was gloriously delusional—I call it the *blindfolded white knight*. I'd plow in, unable to see properly, massively outnumbered, and unaware that the one I was trying to help was about to turn on me and attack. The biggest mistakes I made in this life were those early rescue attempts. They weren't all failures, but most of them were unsuccessful, and the losses I suffered were enormous. I never really got over the memory of them, yet I realized that everyone has to save him- or herself, and although heroism is noble and means well, it's not worth the risk (except in special circumstances).

To summarize, begin by owning your stored pain and make it your brother or sister, and notice the impulses that come up from your subconscious. Processing the pain of your inner child will also help enormously. As the psychological wounds we receive in our youth have been well documented by other authors who are more qualified to write about them than I am, I'll only touch on this topic briefly. Each of us has an abandoned, hurt child within—even if you were brought up in a marvelously loving family. In the modern era, parents are under a great deal of stress to perform and often work long hours. Their offspring are left behind, emotionally forgotten and alone in their little minds—watching TV and trying to work it out.

In addition, we all have the memory of fear, disappointment, and the trauma of our fall from innocence. That's the moment in your teenage years or early 20s when you had to leave the economic and emotional safety of home and stand as a real grown-up, making a living on your own and tending to your needs. Those childhood wounds form part of your innermost recollections because they're part of your stored pain, and you can't get to redemption until you unravel them. If you suffered abuse, I'm sorry that it happened, but you shouldn't let it destroy your life. You could say that anything that didn't kill you is a victory, as it made you wiser and stronger.

At some point you must incorporate a spiritual resolution of that sorrow, and the easiest way is to understand that this journey is so much more complicated than we'll ever know. No one can accurately tell you how you came to suffer the karma of mistreatment and abuse, but the sophisticated way to handle it is not as a perpetual victim, since that will open you up to the darkness of the ghoul worlds. Also, the abuse you suffered is stored in your shadow, and it can make you hard and sometimes call on you subtly to seek vengeance. You might find yourself perpetually angry.

There are a lot of inner-child therapists nowadays, and I went to one several years ago for about six sessions. She was great and helped me see how those wounds of abandonment have driven my life, but in that sadness, I also saw how it helped me because I was frightened into action. I was out and about earning a living at an early age—I didn't have a functional family to rely upon and had to learn to cope quickly. It made me a bit too hard, for I saw life as a threat and had to work on that aspect in order to come back from there and trust in softness.

I think creators and musicians are sometimes troubled because they're tapping into their subconscious mind for their art, and in there they also feel their stored pain—the two are mixed. There's a lot of creative potential deep in your inner self once you travel past the dark, for the sorrow and the flowers are both in the subconscious. I know loads of people who have started a different career late in life once they resolved themselves and touched inside to find something new and fresh. I didn't write my first

book until I was 38. Prior to that I was what I call *self-unemployed,* roaming the streets of London trying to stay out of trouble.

The Presence of Celestial Beings

We're not completely abandoned. There are celestial beings here in this dimension—beautiful ones—and they seem to be coming through the holes in the matrix ever more with each month that passes. But we've found that they don't respond when we're in despair or emotional pain; instead, they back away—either they can't handle it or maybe the emotional bend in our etheric field forces them to retreat.

I know this is going to sound a bit way-out, but they're real. If you're used to reality as a solid affair, then you might be rather skeptical and I'd totally understand your position. But if you ever see the walls go hazy and the floor disappear, then the possibility of an entity walking through from another world doesn't seem odd at all. Here's the story about the ones we first saw while in a castle in the mountains behind Florence, Italy, in May 2001.

The ethereal beings just came through the wall over a period of about 15 minutes as if stepping through cling wrap. It's disconcerting in the beginning to realize that a presence from another world has just appeared in the room—it fries your noodle, but we got used to it. The first time it happened there were more than a dozen people who witnessed it, and the beings stayed for several hours. There were about eight or nine of them. Some were very tall, and they looked like long neon poles with a blue circle at the top. They were so strange yet graceful and evoked bliss by their presence, seeming to provide inspiration in times of need.

In the early days of the Morph, we started seeing other humanlike transdimensional beings, whom I called the *Tall Boys,* even though the first two I ever saw were female. The Tall Boys and Tall Girls radiate a silent power and a dedication that's sacred. They come (I think) from a world (dimension) that's very close to here—a type of heaven that looks similar to Earth. The male beings stand eight to ten feet tall, are extremely good-looking (like models), and can run at about 40 miles per hour. I've never really discovered exactly what they do, as their function is kept secret—we just don't know yet. Sometimes dogs accompany the Tall Boys, and they can also run very fast, acting as etheric guards and watching over humans in case of trouble—especially at night.

Here's an unusual story that I watched in the Morph. A man came to fight in the mountains. He was emotional and unpredictable—a bit of a loose cannon—yet he was strong and resolute and knew a clever trick: that the ghouls use the moon to navigate. Knowing he could never beat the dark beings in a straight fight, the man enticed them to chase him deep into a valley, and then he hid. The ghouls went crazy looking for him! A few days later he reappeared, walking about the hills and whistling like he owned the joint. The ghouls rushed toward him, and he disappeared. This went on for a long time—weeks and weeks—and more ghouls were lured into the trap. The man had charts and knew that an eclipse of the moon was coming. On the night that the moon went dark, all of the entities became very disoriented. They were offered a rotation in hyperspace that temporally blinded them, so they couldn't work out which way was up or how to escape the valley. In the confusion, a superior force arrived and the ghouls got whacked in an electromagnetic way that I have no understanding of, but it's a bit like the ivory tower falling except much stronger.

The ghouls took a terrible bashing, and it wasn't until the moon went bright again quite awhile later that they could gather themselves and retreat from the valley with one shoe on and their knickers in their handbag. All of that occurred in Scotland in November 2002 near Loch Awe—there was definitely a bit of shock and awe that night! I know about it because I was only 20 miles away at the time in a beautiful place called Kilmelford, and the Morph showed me. When it was over and the dust settled, the Tall Boys and dogs started dropping into 3-D in droves. I'll never forget the day: I saw four of the boys, accompanied by two etheric dogs, speeding down a road. They ran four abreast with the dogs slightly behind, and I estimated that they were traveling at 40 to 45 miles per hour. I had no idea where they were headed, but they looked very impressive because of their height and how gracefully they moved, almost effortlessly.

I saw visions of the Tall Boys on and off for a year and a half, but they eventually dropped from view at the end of 2003. These beings are so full of love and calm—they instantly make you feel safe.

Up until recently, I had never actually seen Tall Boys in real life, only visions of them. Then in November 2005, I saw them for the first time here on Earth, so to speak. I was moved, and the whole concept of the Tall Boys became evermore true. There were five or six (I can't quite remember), standing together between a group of palm trees near a beach. They're much taller than how they appeared in my early visions—I'd say they stand 12 to 14 feet high. Their presence is imposing, and I was intrigued that they push away our 3-D reality, giving the impression that they're standing in a hole marked by a dotted line along the edge of their energy body. You feel as if you could walk right through them and arrive at eternity. They seem to straddle a threshold between two worlds.

The night I saw the Tall Boys, they were standing kind of in a circle about seven yards away from me and facing the opposite direction for the most part. They were silently communicating with each other, making slight body movements; each was very slow and calm. There's something stunningly beautiful and majestic about these beings, and they seem to be waiting and watching over humanity at the same time. I reckon they come from a dimension that's located 90 degrees from us because at first I could only view them in my peripheral vision, but as the sight of them settled onto my perception, I could observe them looking straight on.

Luckily they didn't come over to me, which was a good thing, as I'm not quite ready. They're too vast for me to properly comprehend—I need more time, although they're full of dignity and honor, and I felt safe the night that I saw them. They remained for over an hour, then I couldn't see them anymore, but that doesn't mean they were gone—perhaps my perception faded. Among the mayhem of human tyrants and all the ugliness of this world, there's a love and warmth here to help us along, and the way to stay in touch with it is to become warm in your heart and noble like they are.

On the night that I saw the boys, there was another being with them: a female but not a Tall Girl. This one was also very tall but less humanlike, and she was beautiful and feminine, with a long body made of light, similar to the beings we saw in Tuscany. Although she seemed to be connected to the Tall Boys, she looked different and stood a little way off. I found her mysterious and graceful and watched her for more than an hour. To refer to this entity as a pole of light isn't fair, as she was way more radiant, but she was long and thin—utterly celestial. If she had arms, I couldn't see them. She was angelic in the aspects of her feelings. It's wonderful that there are transcendental beings on Earth, otherworldly visitors from a parallel dimension. That's a good thing, for we need all the help we can get, and we should be eternally grateful for it.

The idea that animals such as dogs are in the mirror-world and have an afterlife is strange to think about, but it seems to be true, which is nice. I like them a lot. I love the way they smile—you can't really see it, as it's more in the feeling they give off. Certainly in the early days after Scotland, the etheric dogs appeared in great numbers. We first saw them in the mirror-world, but then they somehow came over here, and we witnessed them in 3-D. I remember coming out of an elevator in a hotel in Austria, and there in the hallway was a massive German shepherd in etheric form sitting just outside of my room. It stayed there all night until dawn. Anytime we were under serious ghoul attack, the dogs showed up; and they still help me, offering security in edgy times. I'm grateful for them, but it seems that the dogs and the Tall Boys are from a realm that's outside of the symmetry of this solid world. If you've ever wondered why God can't come and rescue us, it's because higher angelic beings couldn't get in here. They've been stuck for a long time, but now that might have changed, and some are here to redress the balance.

(I wrote about them in my book *God's Gladiators*.) It's part of the final rescue of humanity.

Some individuals have reported that the transdimensional beings have performed medical operations on them when they were suffering from an ailment. The procedures take place in the etheric and are very distinct, sometimes lasting several hours, and the participants feel the result in their physical body. I think it's like those healers who remove impediments and alleviate sicknesses that often appear as lumps of dark or black in the etheric field.

A friend of mine had a chronic injury in her hip from being a ballet dancer, and she told me that four years ago, a group of women dressed with head scarves appeared to her from another world. They placed long golden needles in her hip, and they also had certain herbal remedies with them that they brought from inner space. When she came out of the session many hours later, her hip was healed and has never troubled her since. I believe that medicine could soon achieve a higher level, for healing in the etheric body might be a major advance in our knowing. In all the mayhem of our world, the final redemption and cure is also here. The rescue is under way—it's wonderful to contemplate!

Thirty years ago my old teacher told me that when things get very tough on Earth, human initiates would appear to help people and take them to safety. He said that we'd arrive in a sacred, noble place—an invisible dimension inside this world—much like the legend of Findley and Camelot. He went on to say that the process of coming into one of these magical parallel realms was no more difficult than walking across a room while removing your overcoat. (He was right.)

The Invisible Man

Now here's an intriguing thing. I've said before that the Morph dematerializes the body, but I'd only ever viewed partial dematerializations, and although I've witnessed that 500 times or more, I had never seen a person disappear completely until recently. One night I encountered the Tall Boys in a garden, and many people were present. One man was standing by a little campfire smoking a cigarette. As I watched him, he started to blip in and out of this reality, but what was so compelling was that his cigarette stayed solid in this reality—it didn't dematerialize! So I could observe it hover in midair as the man moved about. I couldn't see him, of course, but I knew where he was because of the red glow of the cigarette in his hand.

The man dematerialized completely a total of four times. The first three instances were short—less than a minute each—and then he blipped back into view. The last occurrence took place when he was walking across the lawn. Still smoking his cigarette, he vanished between one stride and the next and was gone for about ten minutes. The sight of the cigarette moving about the garden convinced me that I wasn't hallucinating or imagining it. (Since I saw him blip out that night, it's happened one more time to another man I know who's a healer—several people witnessed it.)

That night in the garden I got the feeling that the Tall Boys were showing us what's up ahead. How my ol' teacher knew of these things 30 years ago is a big mystery, but I believe that much of today's happenings have been in the works for a long time. We live in a wonderful age—what's possible and available to us now is a thousand times greater than ever before. Through redemption we can begin to call these magical worlds toward us.

Let's go to the next chapter. I'd like to talk about your role as a magical healer, which comes from the evolution of your resolved soul and your superknowing.

CHAPTER SIX

YOUR ROLE AS THE MAGICAL HEALER

People who find themselves at the bottom of the tower (meaning that it either collapsed or they've fallen off the roof) are affectionately known as the *lunatics on the grass,* but they gradually heal from the trauma, let go, and take to real spiritual ways. The transition may take several years, and during that time they usually drift about experimenting and discovering themselves. Eventually they arrive sideways at what's sometimes referred to as the *zero point.* You'll recall that the tower is constructed of illusions that are held up, in part, by the bioelectricity of the ego. When the zero-point man or woman encounters the ivory tower of another person, he or she can act as the magical healer without anyone ever knowing it. That's because the healer becomes a grounding rod for the discharge of energy and weakens the ego's force. It's a flash of electricity coming off the tower, passing through the zero-point person, and going back into the earth—it's a form of deliverance.

Once you've sorted your fears and your tower has crumbled, you've embraced a bit of humility and thought about service and purpose in life, you've made peace with your dark little brother or spooky younger sister, and you've incorporated the memory of ancient pain into your shield rather than having it victimize you, then you're ready for a future as a magical healer. When you get to none—nil, zero!—all that you'll ever have to do to evoke healing is touch things, breathe on them, or just walk past them. Deepak Chopra once told me that there are still molecules of the breath of Jesus in every square meter of air we breathe. Your imprint stays forever, as far as I understand; it's on the handle of a door you touched ten years ago. That's why people will sometimes walk into a field in the countryside and see a battle that occurred there hundreds of years ago—the imprint remains.

As you silently change things in your heart, the symmetry of your energy will start flowing in the right direction and will flatten out like a plate. The imprint of the world around you will transform to reflect your new resonance, and you'll soon realize that it was all backward . . . like I said it was. You'll see that you haven't come to raise people up—far from it. In a spiritual sense, your function will be to collapse them, for that's the gift of love you offer. The tower comes down, releasing individuals from the torment of it, and they land on the ground where the potential of the authentic self exists. No one ever makes it by going up. It's never been done, and none of the "going up" people will survive—not one. "Up" is yang and it must transmute to yin by going sideways toward it.

You may say, "Steady on, guy. What do you mean 'none'?" And I'd ask if you remember the hotel lobby and the revolving door. Well, imagine that there's a very important lady in the lobby—she's rich and famous and she's on TV, say, so she has many observers and lots of electricity. Now she's heard that there's an immortality that lies beyond the door and will probably be dressed as an "ism": Boo'd-ism, Catholic-ism, Zion-ism, Hindu-ism, green-juice-enemas-up-ya-Pilates-ism—whatever. The lady doesn't know about particle spin, so the door will whirl her around and spit her back out, but there's another small problem. She's carrying an etheric scaffolding pole ten feet high and encrusted with diamanté. It's the symbol of her ivory tower and describes the yang nature of her self-importance. It won't fit in the revolving door or the side door either, and she won't let go of the pole, as her whole life is entrusted to it—and anyway, she bought it on Rodeo Drive, and it cost a slew of *buckeroolies*.

It's not that she's evil necessarily; it's just that the pole is a symbol of her materialism. How will she throw down the weight of it and walk away, shuffling sideways? She usually can't—it's an invisible "pole tax." She'll die trying to get out of the revolving lobby door, banging at it with everything she can muster. But the pole will be waiting for her in the mirror-world as an extra weight, because what you are at the moment of death is what you'll see of yourself when you get over to the other side (and deathbed recantations and last-minute apologies score for little). *You are what you are.* You're all that's contained in the authentic you: the good, bad, or ugly.

In the evolution of zero-point women or men, the pole dissolves and is replaced with anonymity. There's no medicine, as holding your hand is their remedy. Zero-point individuals have no "ism"; they're shuffling sideways toward a deeper awareness. They have no special tricks or feelings of superiority, for they cherish an absence of self and make remembering their only wisdom. They have no plan or scheme because forgetting to die is their motto. And they have no shield or physical self, as their little brother or sister provides protection and a spark of the God-force makes up their body. Zero-point people have no resolution—listening to the rain is their resolve.

Can you see now? Doesn't it feel different? Do you sense the power of backward, and didn't you almost die crying at night in your bed trying to go farther "up"? It was a bit futile—sorry about that. It's our karma to go the wrong way because that's how this matrix is organized. And remember that all information and even spiritual-ism—especially spiritual and metaphysical insight, I'd say—is heavily doctored and controlled by news and propaganda, as that kind of gnosis could allow you to escape. But how much of it tells you, "Sideways, bubba, sideways . . . let's make a run for it!"? Not much. Mostly it signs you up for dogma and locks you in. It's all the power of the matrix for the most part—feeding off people, con-trolling them, and taking them up the garden path the wrong way. Funny, eh? Sad . . . what can one do?

Remember that Jesus ascended sideways—put that on ya fridge lest you forget! I should tell you here that I'm not so clever myself, for it was only the arrival of the Morph lighting it all up that enables you to see the truth. Although I must say that I had an inkling—decades ago—that it was all wrong, but as Morpheus said in the film, the doubt was a splinter in my mind, an irritation. I couldn't work it out, and no one can show it to you. You have to bring down the ivory tower (and/or take the red pill) and go the other way to see for yourself. You also must pray and be unpretentious so that the Great Spirit and the beings here can offer assistance, but anything less than humble and you're up the pole or it's up you—one of the two, tee-hee!

Becoming Part of the Divine Order

People talk of a divine order, which is correct in my view, but usually they refer to it in the context of closing a real-estate deal or finding a soul mate, and that might not be quite as accurate. For all of the spirit beings and digital gods that I've encountered in the celestial worlds, I've never met one who knew anything about romance or the Multiple Listing Service. The heavenly order that's manifested here on Earth is Gaia, which I've spoke of earlier. The planet has a mind, a superknowing, just as we do. In other words, it's an evolving spirit like you and me.

Gaia says that the earth knows how to correct and heal itself, and so as far as I can tell, the divine order that people talk about is the rightness of things, the natural healing of the world. It's where aberrations in the digital, fractal mathematics of reality are put back together again and rebalanced. In essence, I'd say that Gaia is the long-term will of the feminine principle, the goddess. It's the width or breadth of her soul, her desires; and once you become soft and enter into the formula of her spirit (into the higher perception), you become part of the magic. Then you realize that the divine plan is vast and feminine. So there *is* a heavenly force guiding your life, and you'll feel its subtle power when you're very still.

Once you join her, she talks to you and reveals her world. I've seen and documented over 30,000 full-color visions in the last five years—sometimes they come in at the rate of 150 per day! Most have been about the goddess (Gaia and dimensions) and the rebalancing of the planet, but some involve the destiny of humankind. Softness and a gentle eye are the keys. I find it fascinating that books and films are appearing at regular intervals to help us along, not just the *Matrix* movie—which is almost all true, according to what's in the Morph, anyway—but also novels such as *The Da Vinci Code,* which examines ancient scriptures and discovers that Mary Magdalene was a disciple of Jesus's. (She was close to him, and some believe that she was his wife. The Gospel of Mary within the Dead Sea Scrolls states that Jesus kissed her a lot. So even if they weren't married, she must have been a good mate—someone he trusted.)

The Lady of the Lake

The arrival of the goddess is all part of the rebirth of the feminine power, returning to her place in the Trinity. Father, Son, and Holy Mother makes good sense to me, but I don't know about Father, Son, and Holy Ghost—all the ghosts I've met on the path have been ghouls! Anyway, I started to figure out this goddess thing before the Morph showed up in 2001, and I went to Ireland to look for the Lady of the Lake because the myth states that she carried the wounded men across the water through the mist to Avalon. (And I was as knocked about and etherically injured as it gets without capitulating.) I already knew that the myth wasn't fiction—it was the truth, because by then I'd seen the door even though I hadn't been through it yet. If the door is real, then so is Camelot, as the two are connected. So making peace with the feminine seemed like a good tactic, especially for a young lad who didn't know if he was Arthur or Martha. I didn't have a clue—I was as green as freshly picked zucchini.

By the lake I had a near-death experience that was a bit spooky, and I thought I was a goner—ever so slightly dead. I spontaneously popped out of my body as I was walking along and then realized that I was hovering over it about six to ten feet in the air. That wasn't what I had planned! After a few minutes, I couldn't find my physical self at all, and then I lost my sight and got very scared. There was a lad there whom we call the Boy Angel—he was soft and kind. I explained that I couldn't locate my body nor could I see properly; and he told me in a gentle, lilting voice that I had been blinded in this life by importance. I had an inkling that he was right, but I was far too terrified and confused to get into the finer points of transpersonal psychology and that sort of stuff. So I just followed the cadence of the boy's voice, and it gradually led me to the water's edge, where he helped me wash my face. Then I came back to Earth with a clunk. My tower had fallen over!

Life never looked the same after that, for I saw the divine plan. And although I didn't find the Lady of the Lake on that occasion, she eventually found me. She appeared one day—I saw the queen and the Grail, but like Perceval I wasn't allowed to keep it and had to journey through my anguish and sorrow as he did. Anyway, at the lake I learned that all masculine things are "up": The penis is up and so is the ego, self-importance, the tower, intellectual ideas, money, competitive sport, war, politics, and the forces of control. The media are often smarmy hypocrites, and they sustain up as holy and good. But deliverance is down, across, and feminine.

If there is a supreme being, it's female, meaning that the grace of creation is feminine, and that's why I think that God isn't a person necessarily, but the splendor of the God-force in all things: the colors, spark, aliveness, and symmetry . . . it's her. All of us (and even Ka) are inside the goddess, the Lady of the Lake, as she is vast. We're within her in the sense that the balance of Gaia is the master design, and there's a spirit describing our lives, our divine order; and anytime we're going toward harmony and the feminine, we're traveling according to (and inside of) the plan. When we're in the masculine way, we may well be ever so slightly approaching disaster because it's not built to last.

After my experience at the lake, I made a shrine to the feminine spirit, the goddess, in my heart—and you should, too, or perhaps build a little one in your house if the idea isn't weird and uncomfortable. Right now it's wise to hedge your bets because there's no evidence for God the Father (or any male god) in the Morph, beyond the door, or in the celestial or fractal worlds—none, zip, zero! That might be a hard one for you to wrap your head around, but why would I lie? I wouldn't, would I—for what purpose?

Instead there's a mass of evidence for the feminine— not necessarily a goddess in human form, such as Shiva or Kali. I can't vouch for that, but I can attest to the female principle. Now the Bible says that the woman came from the rib of man, but what if it's backward? What if men believe they're ruling the world, but it's actually the feminine spirit that's running the show? She may not have run it here on Earth in the past, but the celestial beings have arrived and she's definitely in charge now.

You might ask, "How does this give me a defined benefit, Stuie?" And I'd answer in all honesty that it may not give you instant gratification, but it might make you very excited because you can turn and go the right way, knowing that it could save you from an upcoming collapse. The world of yang doesn't have much further to go, as thousands of the visions in the Morph deal with variations of a theme that describe the unraveling of the systems that men built. Eventually the entire Western world may fall apart. Maybe the planet can't handle the frenetic activity and consumption because that's yang, but sitting still and conservation is yin. We live in a self-correcting universe where energy seeks to balance itself all the time. Whatever happens, we have to change a bit and become more loving and caring and soft, for if we do, we befriend nature once again and become safe.

Perhaps the Morph arrived when it did because it's here to preside over the changes so that humanity sees the answer and starts to head in the right direction. The plan is vast: It's the interlacing of invisible celestial dimensions with our 3-D world. If you spend time in silence, you'll realize this and know your part in it. You'll hear the buzz and experience the digital downloads that I talked of, but you also must embrace the feminine and make her important. Relax, wait, and trust, understanding that the softness isn't a woman's version of masculine ideas and his lifestyle, where she accommodates his ideas in order to become a sporty, pushy type like him—no, that's not the right way. Many modern ladies think that they're feminine because they have womanly bits and pieces, and they put forth a glamorous mask to show themselves off to their best advantage. There's nothing wrong with that, but it's more of an energy thing, and avoiding the hard, intimidating world of the masculine helps a whole bunch. Femininity has only partly to do with womanhood and everything to do with the polarity of backward, the quality of your imprint . . . snowflake or hellish?

It's best to be less busy, hard, and emotional, as you'll become the unseen current that flows deep underwater.

You can change the world simply by walking past people—not much action is needed. Be patient and know that it's all going in the right direction; and if you're beautiful, kind, and tender, you enlist the power of the plan, for you *are* the plan, and struggling against it is a recipe for more trouble. There's little you have to do: Just go the other way and genuinely try to remember. You should also raise your energy, which is the act of getting rid of stuff, such as your spouse, maybe—just kiddin'. Mainly you need to simplify your life and learn the value of the gentleness of spirit. Doing too much hurts, and I'm sorry if you're in pain. Some individuals may find this goddess thing hard to understand, but it's a backward mind-set. What you didn't do in life sometimes becomes as important as what you did.

The Power of Embracing the Feminine

Okay, let's review: If you handle your stored pain, go through the three liberations, and bypass the need to carry your story like a cross, then you become free and more simple. That's enormously inspirational to other people and becomes a mystery to them. They'll be drawn to you in droves because you'll be the only one in the neighborhood who isn't spiritually crumpled like a pickled walnut. Your clarity will attract lost souls, and complete strangers will start telling you their life story at the supermarket. You may have experienced it already. You can become the magical healer, and while you're getting used to it, tell them what you think, but in the end you'll know that holding their hand is probably all they'll ever need.

If they sense that magic and ask, "What do you do?" You can reply by saying, "I'm an electrician of sorts. Have you heard of the ivory tower?" Eventually you'll be able to put your hand inside of someone's etheric body and pinch a bit cancer out of there before the individual passes the frozen-peas section. He or she won't even have realized what happened! Trust me—I've done it, albeit just once, but that means it's possible in the end. All of these prizes will be gifted to us and stay forever . . . well, maybe not for eternity, but as long as we agree to remain here.

Let me whiz through a handful of ideas, and maybe you can jot down some of them in your dream journal that I mentioned earlier. Take notice if the feminine spirit starts to talk to you through your dreams and visions, for it's beneficial to enter into a meaningful dialogue with her and imagine getting into a permanent relationship. If you turn and face her, there's a great love waiting. She's the "One," in my view.

I've already mentioned some of this elsewhere, so bear with me and I'll go quickly. You need alkalinity in your body and not acidity, which causes disease. Cancer can't survive without it. Go for alkaline foods and surroundings (soft furnishing and colors). The fastest way to change the pH factor in your blood is to add a squeeze of lemon juice into a glass of clean water—strange, eh? You'd normally think that lemons are really acidic, but they increase your alkaline level.

Every meal you eat kills you a little bit more. Research shows that mice that were given a low-calorie diet lived 15 percent longer than the ones that chowed down at the regular rate, so the more food you consume, the more acidity you add to your body. Most vegetarian diets are alkaline (especially raw-food ones) but if you do eat meat, never mind—it's fine. Just go easy on it and try to reduce your intake of other fats and dairy products.

You need balance in your life. Stress isn't compulsory: It's just you fighting to establish or sustain your ego's opinion as to what's supposed to happen, or it results from trying to conform to someone else's demands. Maybe you can change that and become freer. Sometimes too much activity comes from the desire to be important or wanted . . . take a nap instead. Cities are acid; and forests, water, and mountains are alkaline. You need less thinking and more feeling, and don't bother to work it out because the divine plan doesn't follow any logic we understand. In every situation ask yourself, *How does it feel?* Bag too much thinking—it's for amateurs, really!

Stay neutral as much as possible, for benevolence is feminine and antagonism is masculine. If you can't manage compassion, then be less forthcoming with your opinions, as they're probably loads of rubbish that you heard someplace and adopted as your own. There's no need to be combative. Allow others to go first and let them win, pushing, shoving, and talking. Silence is feminine. If people demand to be right, tell them that they are as often as they need to hear it—even if they're wrong. But if they want to fight, walk away because that's safer and more spiritual. Live and let live. Adore everyone and especially praise your tormentors, as they're teaching you things, such as *Go the other way!*

Be modest because you can never have enough humility, and it's the alkaline version of your soul. You never really need to push yourself up or boast to get over people, to be one better. Agree to be less, while feeling fine about yourself, and step to the back of the line. If you're balanced, you won't be in a rush, anyway. Embrace everyone and exclude no one, but that doesn't mean you have to carry home every deadbeat you meet, feeding and providing for them and so forth. However, don't knock them down or emotionally reject them, either. Build them up and be encouraging. Make them right, even if they seem to be acting a bit weird.

Be grateful, appreciative, and less demanding—and I don't just mean a passing nod. Really try to feel it in your heart, the blessing of the people you know, their presence, and the joy of the gifts you receive. Be genuinely thankful for every small mercy. I'm always shocked by how people have so little gratitude for life and the things that they're given, but it's the arrogance of ignorance once more. Listen! It's a bloody miracle you survived the night, as anything could have happened. Isn't it bloody marvelous that you're still here and you have a few friends and relatives who love you in spite of your faults and how you might have treated them? Appreciate it—show it and mean it and say so, acting from your heart. This is spiritual and considerate, while demanding that everyone provide for and support you is masculine and often disrespectful. It's the ethereal brat hoping to intimidate the world into a free ride.

Try to donate money to worthy causes; and if you aren't rich, then give of yourself by offering a warm word, a kind sentiment, or a helping hand. Put forth your energy and care for everyone. (It's about giving and not taking, remember, and saving, not using.) Watch what you consume and start to use less. Think about this: Buy a bag of rice and pour it into seven cups—not big coffee mugs, just regular-sized teacups. Then get three onions and cut each one in half so you'll have six equal portions. Next week boil one cup of rice per day and eat that with a half of onion, and that's it . . . nothing else.

Of course, on the seventh day you won't have any more onions, but that's good because it will remind you how utterly wonderful they are, and you'll be grateful for them. At the end, you'll learn to consume less, and you'll be so happy for the variety of food and delicacies that were placed on your table in this life. The flip side is mostly a voracity of consumption and looks ugly (you don't need the half of it). Try this and you'll see it all for what it is and learn to be grateful for even a small amount of rice and an onion. It was good, you'll say—the rice-and-onion week.

Now if you have any illnesses or are likely to suffer from Stuie Wilde's patented Rice-and-Onion Exercise, then consult your health-care practitioner, as they say in American television ads. If you don't fancy the rice and onions, then try something else: Turn off the TV for a week, attempt a day of complete silence, or deprive yourself of something that you're used to always having. If you like going around in your car, take the bus or walk for a week, and you'll become aware of how grateful you are for having a vehicle in your life.

Being is better than doing, as it's during the quiet time that you feel the impulses we discussed in previous chapters. Individuals think that they have free will, but they're only responding to those urges from within. Free will is mostly an illusion: You get up and make coffee without deciding to do so, and before you know it, you're in the kitchen (reacting to that inner prompt). If you smoke, you're aware of how suddenly there's a cigarette in your hand, and you realize that you lit it without being cognizant of it. We're pushed from the inner world, and that's why that deeper being must become authentic; otherwise, we travel away from softness and spirituality

toward a harsh reality where we'll eventually get hurt in the darkness of a global crunch.

The Final Crunch

We live in the strangest of times. Because of TV, the global mind is externally exhibited in that we can see what others are thinking and doing, and we know what's happening all 'round the world. We've come to trust the broadcasters whom we tune in to every night, but what we're told by the media is tainted by the party line, the official view. The networks massage the stories, yet the selling of the big lie is a manifestation in the construct of the matrix. The lies are the knots that hold the net together.

Each of our nations has an inner identity, a collective self, and you can see how deep that goes and how difficult it is for some to exit that mind-set. Within it, we're traveling at the speed of light toward the edge of a cliff—the ice is melting, penguins are wearing sunglasses, storms lash the coasts, and so on. Governments are blind to reality because it's all about politics, donations, black money, and power trips. It's the ego's big erection, but we're running out of Viagra to hold it all up. To put it simply, humanity is heading toward the biggest crunch in history, and that's why backward will eventually save your little butt. Soon you must jump out of the global karma, as it's on the verge of a social and political tsunami. If you're a sensitive person and already perceive the wobble, you're feeling the matrix cracking up. In other words, the guards in the hotel lobby with the revolving door are starting to go ever so slightly mad and are losing control over the guests. Security is prancing up and down in pink fishnet tights doing the funky chicken. The system is going berserk, as the hairline fracture in our collective soul widens. Go to love!

Here's how it will help you: When I saw the Tall Boys and the dogs in Scotland, I didn't know what they meant, but they were the forerunners of spiritual beings coming through a crack in reality. Since that time, we were shown how the opening has gotten bigger, and eventually millions poured in—not just Tall Boys and etheric dogs, but great spirits, such as archangel-type beings. They're here, not to fight the dark, but to encircle it and cut it off from its power base, degrading it to impotency. This means that places are being cleared, and when the ghouls are ejected from an area, the human tyrants fall because they're powerless without the darkness holding them up—weird, but true.

That's why the promise of the scattered Camelots (dimensions that people can hide in) is being realized. There are places in the world you can retreat to—mini-heavens that aren't visible to the naked eye. One is located in Switzerland near Morgins, another is in the Austrian Tyrol, and there's a possibility of one at Crested Butte in Colorado. To find them, you need to develop the same Camelot-style feeling in your heart, and that's what we've been chatting about in these pages. It's grace and deliverance, gratitude and service, and of course, humility.

(*Traveler's advisory:* Don't be rushing off for Morgins just yet, as the door is only 18 inches long and 4 inches wide, and it's hovering about 30 feet above the ground. The one in Colorado may not appear for nine years or so.)

You'll take shelter in your heart, traveling through it to another world. There's no separation because everything is connected. It's vast and will guide you, but you don't need to head for the hills and buy canned food—you could hide in downtown Detroit. You're a universe unto yourself. If you're an ugly one, you'll be aligned with the predators and ghouls and they'll eventually come and claim you, but if you've turned to beauty (even a little) and you've gone from cold to warm and become an authentic human, then you can have your own mini-Camelot in your living room if you'd like.

The door is right here. Put your arms out and look at the end of your fingers, as three to four feet from them is where the otherworld begins. It's the gap in the ceiling of the gymnasium that you can disappear into. On 9/11 when the Twin Towers fell in New York City, that was a major sign of the beginning. The towers represented the peak of commerce and yang power, and they symbolized a world power force—a secret one—and our collective karma. The global madness brought them down, as it's the start of the ivory tower crumbling. America and its allies were suckered into war and massive debt, but it's all part of the plan to bring us down and not up, and all of that won't affect you as long as you're not too far on the *upside* of things.

In the Morph, I observed many visions of the future that eventually did take place and others that also seemed to come true. For example, I viewed that Yasir Arafat (the former Palestinian leader) had died, and I saw a bullet in a cup. I thought that meant he would be poisoned—he did succumb to a mysterious blood disease—but the theory hasn't been proven conclusively, so some of the visions remain an enigma. However, many of the Morph visions happened, and some of them were curiously wrong. One instance of this was when I saw the tsunami hit the northern part of the Pacific on November 6, 2004, but it struck 50 days later and 12,000 miles away in Sumatra . . . that was very strange.

Even when the information is slightly inaccurate or misunderstood, the overall theme doesn't seem to waver much, so it leads me to think that we're living inside a renewal—not the destruction of the universe necessarily, but maybe the end of the world as we know it. It has to include a spiritual resolution for you, me, and all of humanity; and it must come with forgiveness, goodness, and love, not condemnation or vengeance. It took me a long time to see that.

The softness of the goddess is the only safe way, for she's the one driving the Gaia bus. If you go the other route, you'll be lost, so take note of what you have under your control. In other words, your plan ought to include scaling back and getting smaller, and there's no need to rush or panic, but do start working on simplicity bit by bit. If you can make money and forge ahead without harm, then do so, but you should try to look to your overall well-being. Those who are highly leveraged may find themselves on the beach nibbling burned toast as the tsunami builds out at sea.

Start to see how you might invest in yourself and gain knowledge or a skill or something that you'll use to serve humanity, as that's your way of going sideways. Strive for what's real, true, and uplifting; and stay away from whatever is phony and debilitating. It goes back to our initial discussion on variance.

Then try this: Call to the celestial energies to retrieve you, and do so every night for a few minutes before you go to sleep. Let them know that you need awareness, you want to see, and you're ready and willing to jump or act if needed. (Mobility will help a lot, so become fluid in your feelings—that's what liberation is all about.) I swear that I found the Lady of the Lake because I wanted her more than anything else and was prepared to give up everything to find her. So you decide: Do you want the spiritual path, or will you dither and waver, doing nothing and pretending? Will you jump? If you do take a leap, spirit will come with a new grace to catch you, but you have to act first without knowing if you'll break every bone in your body at the bottom.

There's a world, another dimension that's pure heaven, below us—straight down. It's hard to imagine something celestial there because we've been taught that heaven is above. I call that underneath bliss the *fally-down world,* for it's a strange multidirectional hyperspace. There's no up or down in there, and it's in perpetual rotation, which doesn't allow you to quite work out which way up you are. Anyway, I got there because one day a spiritual entity from the Morph appeared beside me, and I was shown a curtain that looked a bit like a waterfall. He/she/it—whatever the being was—sort of helped me walk though it, and on the other side I twisted, and my right foot went to where my left foot was and vice versa. I started to rapidly drop, as if I were falling from the top of a high office building. After about 50 stories had passed, I suddenly made a sharp right turn at 90 degrees and then kept descending. I was terrified and braced myself for a crushing impact at the bottom, for when you're in those worlds, you can't tell if it's real or not. Your inner etheric self feels just like your physical body—more so, in a way, as it's very sensitive.

At the bottom there was a soft landing and the most wonderful bliss and serenity. I have no idea why I was led to the fally-down world, but I've been there several times since, and I learned that if you let go and trust, it will always be okay. It's only when you hang on that you miss opportunities, and it hurts you a whole lot.

There's a quirky thing in Amazonian shamanism called the Blessing of the Snake that occurs when you consume the sacred brew *ayahuasca*. Suddenly in the middle of a journey through those spiritual worlds, a massive snake appears in your mind's eye (it's like an anaconda) and comes to eat you. The trick is to let it, because beyond the belly of the snake is another heaven. You don't die—you just find yourself in another place, better than before. It's a rebirth, like the renewal that the world is about to go through. You learn to stay calm (and not panic) and let go, allowing the forces to carry you, for they know. You usually don't comprehend and in a way you don't need to, because maybe if you did, you'd stuff it up and change your destiny.

You have to embrace a mind-set of nonresistance. Women don't resist the way men do, and they have a much greater ability to withstand pain, as they're more allowing and passive. In the softness, there will always be someone to love and care for you, because you'll be in the kingdom of God where the heart people dwell. It's only in the yang world of predators and hardness that you'll be shunned and where people may walk over you in the street. Trust that spirit is soft and the snake is soft, and the bottom of the fally-down world is, too. It's all loving in the end if your heart is warm and kind.

The Initiate and the Master Builder

In ancient texts the magical healer was given the number 22 and the master builder was number 11. The master builder knows the sacred mathematics of the golden mean (the spiral geometry that the great pyramid was built around), and it's said that he'll re-create the temple that was destroyed in Jerusalem. I don't think it's meant to be taken literally, as it's more that the master builder holds a sacred space for humankind during the renewal so that they'll have a safe haven to live and evolve—a ghoul-free domain. In the legend, he has a rod with which to make the proper measurements, and it was considered sacred because it was precisely linked to the circumference of the earth and the distance to the moon. In other words, the master builder has a heavenly perspective and understands that we live in a vast geometry with everything interconnected. (Tarot-card readers are joined to the energy of the master builder because of the cryptograms on their cards and the way they're laid out in precise geometric patterns.)

Eventually you're reborn in the void. You are the universe: It's inside you and you're within it. It's minute and vast at the same time, and so are you. You could hold the whole world in your heart once you allow it to expand, keeping a thousand people safe—and 10,000 more if you had the goodness and willingness to do so. Someone will have to do it, and that might be your final offering before you decide to leave. It's the gift of the master builder (or we can say the sacred mother) who protects us in troubled times—nice, eh? If you could manage that, it might be more than you ever expected in this life, as nothing is impossible once you clearly see your way. You can't believe what's coming, but you accept it and get ready.

Perhaps you can use your resources to establish something really fantastic by building or creating a center or space (even a tent in the forest) where people are able to meet and talk about their lives—a place of refuge. The world of the master builder is a specialized energy, but there's an urgent need for such individuals to step up and get going now.

The initiate was given the number 33, and he or she is a shaman who has the power over the nature kingdoms and transdimensional doorways. Initiates know herbs and plant medicines and the great mysteries, and sometimes they move inside the overall imprint of the matrix without the ghouls catching on. They have the power of evasion—I've always been impressed by that, although I found it strange that almost all of the initiates don't know what they are. There are many more of them than you'd imagine, and those I know are anonymous, not famous or obvious. I think that their main function is to carry people across the gap, but they're also linked to the Tall Boys, each having the power of the light and dark. Some would live as if straddled between here and a transdimensional world where there's constant interchange between the ghouls and the forces of good. If you're part of the 33, you might have had an inkling of it, but then again, you may not know it yet. As your energy gets stronger, it all becomes obvious. What it will mean in the end I can't accurately say; and if I took a guess, I'd probably fall far short, for the final plan is well beyond me.

I only know my little bit, and that's not very significant. I've always seen myself as a tracker, discovering the territory and then showing others the way across—the concierge at the side door . . . taxi, anyone? Some of the human initiates who straddle across are commanders of vast armies, inner-world forces that are part of Armageddon, and it's visible in the Morph although we can't work it out yet. But there's a massive movement rising that will encircle the ghouls and rob them of their power base, bringing the tyrants of the world to their knees. Goodness knows how long it will take—many years, I should imagine.

If you're drawn to the initiate's world, then you must be special, and inside you is a formula—a unique icon that identifies who you are—and it would have been there before the universe formed. You have the knowing (more than anything that I could tell you), and you would have seen parts of the plan. Your parts are particular to you, and you would have observed them in your dreams and visions. Maybe you didn't believe them or are waiting for someone to carry you out of where you are, but there's no one coming. *You* are the lifeboat because your energy is faster and wider than anyone else's. If you don't accept your role, no one will be saved. All I can say is that now is the time, so be brave and make your move.

The Mark on the Forehead

We've seen the mark on the forehead that's mentioned in Revelation, and it looks like a vortex of energy, which morphs and moves about just under the hairline. In some individuals it's circular, similar to a small doughnut, and in others it's like a spiral galaxy. People with the mark are important, for they're the initiates, but as far as I can work it out, the mark is almost always hidden. I've only ever seen it on five people, but the power of the 33 will come into its own soon, as it's been said that in the end the initiates will appear and guide humans to safety. I think some realize that they're initiates right away and others get it over time, and what they learn isn't so much in books; rather, the interdimensional downloads teach them.

Digression: You might wonder if there's a mark of the beast, and the answer is yes. I've never seen it in the inner worlds, but I've observed it on humans from time to time. Some people believe that the modern bar codes on products is the mark of the beast because they have a hidden six at the beginning, middle, and end of them (6-6-6). The strange thing is that like a bar code, the evil mark on humans appears as parallel lines usually on the left cheek (although it can be visible anywhere on the face and upper body). In most instances it looks like a tattoo, composed of three black lines that are just over half an inch thick and are on the cheek below the eye in a slanted position. I've never once spoken to an individual who has the mark because they have such an evil vibe. I keep away, as it's more than I care to tackle, and it isn't sensible to take unnecessary risks.

Conclusion

To go back to the sacred numbers, 44 was assigned to the Christ consciousness, the risen God, and the eternal love that surpasses good and evil, suffering, and human life. I don't think we can know much about it, for it's beyond the side door. There's no 55 as far I know and 66 is the devil, which, of course, isn't really accurate, as it's just manifestations of ancient stored pain. I found it interesting that if you add up the numbers of the master builder (11), the magical healer (22), and the initiate (33), their sum is 66; and if you add the Christ consciousness (44) and the magical healer, it also equals 66. So you can surmise that 66 is a combination of the others, a symbol of the aware person who's redeemed and made whole.

After 66 there's the 77, which we believe only arrives once every 10,000 to 15,000 years because it's part of the renewal. It's not a person, but a fluctuation in the stability of the quantum vacuum of the universe. The best way to describe it is to say that it's a burst of light that appears out of nowhere—spontaneous combustion. In theory, there should be nothing there. Strangely the 77 is really the creation of matter/light, and perhaps it represents the very source of all life. In the Morph this number also has an icon or a symbol to describe it, which is a little oblong box (sort of like a brick) with angels' wings—it's really cute. This sacred numeral is more powerful than anything that has ever been seen here before because it's the synapse that takes place when the two worlds meet: the celestial realm and this 3-D world.

Where will it carry us? Out and beyond karma or torment to a safe place—the pain-free zone. It may take us a while to get there, but there's never a rush, so take your time and go as fast or slow as you like.

Here's something quirky to consider, and again I have to go back to the *Matrix* film to explain it. Morpheus thought that Neo was the One, but the rest of his crew weren't completely sure. The people at Zion believed it and began to worship Neo, begging for favors and healing. Trinity trusted it and the Oracle wasn't saying one way or the other, except that Neo was waiting for something.

Throughout the story, Neo doesn't believe it either, but at the end of the trilogy he realizes that he is, indeed, the One, so he embarks on the final journey into the heart of evil in order to save Zion and the human world. It's the reunification all over again. Neo fights the last battle with his little brother (the anti-Neo), represented by the dark Agent Smith, and he allows the evil to come into him and embraces it—the light and dark are joined. The One (Neo) and his opposite (Agent Smith) create an explosion of light, which is a burst of the 77, and the Smith program disintegrates into a thousand pieces, as we watch the dark melt into the light. The squiddies retreat and the human world of Zion is saved. You could say that the 77 is your deliverance, for it's the quantum burst of light that occurs at the final moment of redemption.

Once you believe that you're the savior of yourself (and perhaps a few others), *you* are the One. You're the master builder or the initiate—whatever you decide, and that's what I found so strange and wonderful. There's no one above to point you out or select you, as it's self-selection, anonymous and silent. You determine it without telling anyone.

It's the deliverance, and that's beyond enlightenment, which is just a name for our spiritual process. Redemption is illumination for everyone, for it transports us via the spectacular burst of the 77 through the gap to where enlightenment is irrelevant. The light transcends good and evil, karma, pain, and remorse—it exceeds all normal definitions. It's where you cross the garden and disappear, smoking a cigarette . . . or not, as you wish.

Pick a number: 11, 22, or 33, and then find your dark little brother or devilish sister and make them right and love them. Embrace the softness of the goddess and surrender; and I'll see you at the side door, the one that leads to the blissful heavens I spoke of. Remember, you

don't have to look for the gap because it's everywhere, and ascension is sideways between one side of a beautiful garden and the other.

Thanks, love, love,
Stuie Wilde

ABOUT
THE AUTHOR

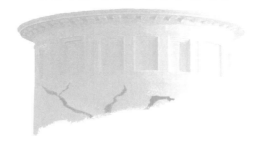

Author and lecturer **Stuart Wilde** is an urban mystic, a modern visionary; he has written 17 books on consciousness and awareness, including the very successful Taos Quintet, which are considered classics in their genre. They are: *Miracles, Affirmations, The Force, The Quickening,* and *The Trick to Money Is Having Some!*

Stuart's perceptive and quirky way of writing has won him a loyal readership over the years. He has a simple way of explaining things that hitherto have seemed a mystery. His books have been translated into 15 languages.

Websites: **www.stuartwilde.com**
and **www.redeemersclub.com**

NOTES

NOTES

NOTES

NOTES

Hay House Titles of Related Interest

Count Your Blessings: *The Healing Power of Gratitude and Love,*
by Dr. John F. Demartini

The Divine Matrix: *Bridging Time, Space, Miracles, and Belief,*
by Gregg Braden

Four Acts of Personal Power: *How to Heal Your Past and
Create a Positive Future,* by Denise Linn

The Healing Power of Water, by Masaru Emoto

Inspiration: *Your Ultimate Calling,* by Dr. Wayne W. Dyer

The Power of Infinite Love & Gratitude: *An Evolutionary
Journey to Awakening Your Spirit,* by Dr. Darren R. Weissman

Soul on Fire: *A Transformational Journey from Priest to Shaman,*
by Peter Calhoun

Spiritual Connections: *How to Find Spirituality Throughout
All the Relationships in Your Life,* by Sylvia Browne

The Times of Our Lives: *Extraordinary True Stories of Synchron-
icity, Destiny, Meaning, and Purpose,* by Louise L. Hay & Friends

Your Destiny Switch: *Master Your Key Emotions, and
Attract the Life of Your Dreams!* by Peggy McColl

All of the above are available at your local bookstore,
or may be ordered by contacting Hay House (see next page).